The Last of the West Country Merchants

Christopher J. A. Morry

Cover Photo

The cover photo is of a portrait of Matthew Morry. But the question of which Matthew Morry is a matter of some debate. Other family historians have concluded that it is Matthew Morry III, the grandson of the man who brought the family from Devon to Newfoundland. This is in part a result of oral history to that effect and in part attributable to the fact that there exist portraits or photos of three of his brothers. However, the clothing worn by the man in the portrait has more the appearance of that worn in the late 18th century, not the mid-19th century, and I am inclined to believe, therefore, that this is a likeness of Matthew Morry (1750- 1836).

The Last of the West Country Merchants

The Life and Times of Matthew Morry (1750-1836), One of the Last Generation of Merchant Adventurers in the Newfoundland Fish Trade, with Notes on His Ancestors in Devon and His Descendants in Newfoundland and Around the World

Christopher J. A. Morry

Avalonia & Hibernia Enterprises
4-160D Edwards St.
Rockland, Ontario K4K 1H9
www.avalonia-hibernia.ca

Copyright © 2019 Christopher J. A. Morry
Library and Archives Canada Cataloguing in Publication
Morry, Christopher, 1949-, author

The Last of the West Country Merchants: The Life and Times of Matthew Morry (1750-1836), One of the Last Generation of Merchant Adventurers in the Newfoundland Fish Trade, with Notes on His Ancestors in Devon and His Descendants in Newfoundland and Around the World / Christopher J. A. Morry.
ISBN 978-1-7753535-0-8 (Bound)
ISBN 978-1-7753535-1-5 (eBook)

1. Matthew Morry, 1750-1836 - Biography. 2. Newfoundland Cod Fishery, 18th and 19th Centuries – Personal Narratives. 3. Newfoundland Merchants – History. 4. Dartmouth, Devon, England – Personal Narratives. 5. Caplin Bay (Calvert), Newfoundland – Personal Narratives. 6. Ferryland, Newfoundland – Personal Narratives.

Previous page: *Matthew Morry's first application for a grant of a fishing room in Caplin Bay (now Calvert), 1784, Provincial Archives Division, The Rooms Corporation, St. John's, MG237 Box 1 File 8.*

All Rights Reserved. No part of this publication may be reproduced, stored in a retrieval system or transmitted, in any form or by any means, without the prior written consent of the publishers or a license from The Canadian Copyright Licensing Agency (Access Copyright). For an Access Copyright license, visit www.accesscopyright.ca or call toll-free to 1-800-893-5777.

To the rough and tumble fish

Merchants of the West Country

Who came and stayed,

And to my son Bryan

Whose stay was all too brief

Contents

Preface and Acknowledgements	xiii
Chapter One - Land and Sea	1
Chapter Two – Building the Historical Narrative	6
Some Cautionary Notes	8
The Path Ahead	15
Chapter Three – Early Roots In Stoke Gabriel	17
The Earliest Known Members of Matthew Morry's Family	17
Stoke Gabriel in the 16th and 17th Centuries	22
William Mory (ca 1624-1692)	30
John Mory (1663-1736)	31
Chapter Four - The Transition Years	37
John Morey (1687-1772)	37
Chapter Five - The Dartmouth-Newfoundland Connection	43
Dartmouth's Past	43
The Early Days of English Fishing and Settlement in Newfoundland	46
Dartmouth in the Early 18th Century	55

John Morey (1711-1751)	58
Chapter Six - Striking Out For Parts Unknown	**62**
Matthew Morry I (1750-1836)	62
Matthew Morry I's Rise as a Merchant Mariner (1771-1774)	86
Matthew Morry & Co. (1775-1813)	91
Chapter Seven – Court Cases Involving Matthew and John Morry	**102**
Introduction	102
His Majesty's High Court of Chancery	104
His Majesty's Court of King's Bench	114
The Supreme Court of Newfoundland	118
Questions and Answers Concerning Court Records	123
Chapter Eight - Caplin Bay and Ferryland	**129**
A Brief History of the Fishery in Ferryland and Caplin Bay	129
The Seasonal Fishery Years	133
Matthew Morry and his Second Wife, Anne Carter	142
The Morrys of Caplin Bay and Their Kin	143

Chapter Nine – First Generation Newfoundlanders	156
Matthew Morry II's Family	156
Appendix 1: Lineage Chart of the Author	180
Appendix 2: Family Group Sheets	183
Appendix 3: Court Cases	200
References	205
Author's Biography	211

Table of Figures

Figure 1. A View of Stoke Gabriel on the Dart River   2

Figure 2. Stoke Gabriel, Dartmouth and the River Dart   5

Figure 3. James Yonge Map of Ferryland and Caplin Bay, 1663   8

Figure 4. A Page from Ann Coulman's Bible   10

Figure 5. Anglican Cathedral and St. Thomas's ca 1892   13

Figure 6. An Exeter-Dartmouth Port Book from 1710   16

Figure 7. Stoke Gabriel from Cornworthy across the River Dart 23

Figure 8. St. Gabriel Churchyard, the River Dart Estuary   24

Figure 9. Sandridge Estate, Stoke Gabriel   26

Figure 10. The John Davis Monument in Dartmouth   27

Figure 11. John H. Morry and Holdsworth House, ca 1890   28

Figure 12. Sir Humphrey Gilbert Monument in Dartmouth   29

Figure 13. Baptismal Record of John Mory (1663-1736)   33

Figure 14. The Two Marriages of John Moury/Morey   40

Figure 15. The Grave of Mary Morrey St. Clement Churchyard 46

Figure 16. Arthur Holdsworth ca 1700   50

Figure 17. Ken Peacock and Howard Morry, Ferryland, 1951   53

Figure 18. Higher Street and Foss Street, Dartmouth ca 1800   54

Figure 19. Dartmouth from St. Clement Townstal ca 1900   55

Figure 20. "Prosperity to Hooks and Lines"   58

Figure 21. N. Crewe Note in Volume of William Shakespeare   68

Figure 22. Vol. 3 with Signature of Matthew Morry I   69

Figure 23. Vol. 4 with Signature of Matthew Morry Jr.   70

Figure 24. Vol. 2 of Complete Works of Shakespeare   70

Figure 25. Mary [Graham] Morry's Gravestone, St. Saviour's   72

Figure 26. Two Baptism Records for Honor Moary   75

Figure 27. Auctioning One of John Morry's Prizes   77

Figure 28. Two of John Morry's £3 Per Cent Annuities   79

Figure 29. Matthew Morry's Bible   83

Figure 30. Plan of Ferryland and Capling [sic] Bay 1775   90

Figure 31. A Kingsbridge Bank Note   94

Figure 32. Death of Richard Morry as French Prisoner of War   100

Figure 33. A "Complaint" Filed with High Court of Chancery   123

Figure 34. Matthew Morry Privy Council Appeal   128

Figure 35. Caplin Bay early 20th century   135

Figure 36. Athlone and its Last Occupant Miss Lizzie Morry   141

Figure 37. Sweetland House, Then and Now   141

Figure 38. Silhouette of Lieut. Henry Sweetland, RN   155

Figure 39. Gravestone of Matthew Morry and Grandson   157

Figure 40. Portraits of Four Sons of Matthew II   159

Figure 41. Newman House, 1 Springdale Street, St. John's   161

Figure 42. Memorial to William Sweetland Morry, Aquaforte   163

Figure 43. Mary Morry Le Messurier ca 1850   164

Figure 44. Ann Coulman Winsor ca 1890   166

Figure 45. Howard Morry beside the Holdsworth Stone   167

Figure 46. Ferryland Northside Holdsworth Premises ca 1840   168

Figure 47. John Henry Morry, his Daughters and Niece   169

Figure 48. Gravestone of Sarah Carter, Ferryland Museum   178

PREFACE AND ACKNOWLEDGEMENTS

Let me begin this Preface with a confession: the subject of this book, Matthew Morry, was NOT the very Last of the West Country Merchants[1], as the title of the book may seem to imply. Rather he was one of a distinct category of West Country Merchants who came at the very end of the period in history when Newfoundland's economy was entirely run for the benefit of absentee merchants living in the southwest of England (hence the title generally applied to them as a group). The group of latter-day merchants like Matthew Morry differed in one important respect from their predecessors; they gave up their homes in England and moved to Newfoundland, there to stay and start their mini-dynasties in that new land. This is an important distinction, as I hope to make clear in this book.

---

[1] "West Country Merchant" was a term applied by historians to merchant adventurers from the west country of England, primarily, Devon, Dorset and Bristol, who were the first Englishmen to exploit the rich cod fisheries off Newfoundland.

I only became interested in my family history in 1996, at the age of forty-seven, though for my entire lifetime my grandfather, Howard Leopold Morry (known to the family as Dad Morry) had regaled family members and anyone else who would listen to him with what should have been fascinating stories of the adventures and "derring-do" of many of our ancestors, including characters known as "Red Matt", "Foxy Bob", "Long Will" and others. Like most young people, I let stories like these go in one ear and out the other.

My interest in 1996 was triggered in a curious sort of way. My wife, who was then working for the federal government, received an email from another government employee named Marla Morry in Winnipeg who wondered if her family and ours might be related in some way. It was not an unreasonable assumption, since the surname is rare in Canada, as it is in most of the rest of the world. However, as it turned out, Marla was descended from Russian Jews whilst we were of English Protestant stock as far back as Dad Morry knew. Marla's family believed that their surname came from an ancestor who emigrated to Russia from Scotland, so it is still not certain that we are in no way related, though no link has been found in the subsequent twenty-three years of curiosity-driven, intensive research that this initial encounter triggered.

This book represents only a small part of the results of that research. It focuses almost exclusively on the story of Matthew Morry, the immigrant ancestor who began to come to Newfoundland seasonally in the mid to late 1700s and finally settled there in the early 1800s. Other parts of this research, and the lessons learned from carrying out the research, have already been published or will be published in other forms in the future.

The concept of this book has changed since it was originally conceived about five years ago. Initially, it was intended to be a consolidation of all the information gathered on the family history of the Morry family of Newfoundland (ex-Devon) simply to ensure that this information, gathered over a period of about fifty years, would not be lost and would continue to be available to future generations. The target audience for such a book would be exceedingly small.

As such, the product of this research, conducted originally by my grandfather, Howard Leopold Morry, and to a much larger extent his daughter Jean [Morry] Funkhouser, and then continued by me after her death in 1996, would most likely not constitute a matter of interest to a conventional publisher.

I expect to one day present the results of these combined efforts in the form of a genealogical and family history report in the annals of either the Family History Society of Newfoundland and Labrador or the Devon Family History Society, as I am a member of both.

However, during the course of my own studies on the family's history, a realisation began to emerge. The immigrants of this family who began their careers as migrant fish merchants from the West Country of England, like so many others, but who finally settled in this new country to raise their families and carry on their business ventures, represented a class of merchants not well studied in the history of the settlement and development of Newfoundland. At least their contributions were not as well studied as those of the dominant merchant class families of that part of England who had made fortunes in the Newfoundland cod fishery but then had returned to England to enjoy the benefits of those fortunes.

There was by no means a complete void in the books written on the history of settlement in Newfoundland. But very few of those histories speak of these rugged entrepreneurs at any length. The role played by the small-scale merchants who came from the West Country to Newfoundland and stayed has, therefore, to my observation, not been accorded as much attention as they deserve, considering the important role that they played at the local level in Newfoundland.

There were exceptions, of course. One notable exception was Robert Carter of Ferryland. But he is better remembered because he played a dramatic role in the defence of Newfoundland under attack once again by the French under d'Haussonville during the Seven Years War/French and Indian War in 1762-63 in what became one of the last engagements between the English and French over territory in North America, leading to the Treaty of Paris in 1763. His role as the principal resident merchant and mainstay of the economy on that part of the Southern Shore received much less attention in the history books.

The earlier West County Merchants were predominantly the scions of important merchant class families in England who came to Newfoundland, if at all, only seasonally, returning to the comforts of their country homes in England to avoid the bitterly cold winter months in Newfoundland. As examples of this class of businessmen, one can think of names such as the Newmans, Hunts and Holdsworths. In contrast, the smaller-scale West Country Merchants of whom I speak chose to stay in Newfoundland because of the better opportunities presented for the growth of their family businesses in this new land.

The Morrys and the Southern Shore families into which they intermarried and with whom they conducted business, such as the Winsors[2] of Aquaforte, the Sweetlands of Caplin Bay (now Calvert) and the Carters of Ferryland fell into this latter category. Matthew Morry I[3] was a self-made man who rose initially from an ordinary seaman on voyages to Newfoundland to become the Master of such vessels and then an owner and fish merchant in his

---

[2] Another of those Newfoundland families whose name has been seen spelled in different ways: Winser, Winsor and Windsor - sometimes with multiple spellings applied to indicate the same person.

[3] For clarity, I call him Matthew Morry I because he had a son and grandson of the same name who carried on in the same business after him.

own right in a remarkably short period of time in the mid to late 1700s.

The plan, therefore, began to form in my mind that by focussing on telling the story of Matthew Morry and his kin I would be adding a little at least to provide a better balance of treatment to what I consider to be two distinctly different categories of West Country Merchants.

The many fine histories of Newfoundland (see References) that have been written chose to focus mainly on the initial settlement, as sponsored by the fishing operations managed by the larger merchant families in the 17th and 18th centuries. At that point, invariably their attention was drawn to the important matter of nation-building and the drive for responsible government in the 19th century. In the process, not as much attention was dedicated to the more mundane ongoing struggles of the people in the outports to make a living from the fishery and related shipping enterprises during this era. Though the story may have seemed less dramatic and probably less important to some historians, it is nevertheless the story of how the nation survived during these years of political and economic upheaval and change and is well worth telling in greater detail. Other observers have come to a similar conclusion. Robert Cuff, in a paper he presented to Provincial Historic Commemorations Program in November 2014 (see References) had this to say:

> *"In their impact on Newfoundland and Labrador's economic development, patterns of settlement, and community life, 19th-century outport merchants made a significant historic contribution.*
> *Their secondary impact, on the Province's political and cultural development, may be less obvious but was nonetheless vital. Each merchant had a demonstrable impact beyond his home community, in that each supplied nearby communities. Although a merchant's commercial home sphere was typically*

in the headquarters bay or region, the majority of the outport merchants were also involved in both fishing and in supplying planters/fishers in migratory or vessel-based fisheries elsewhere: the Labrador and French Shore fisheries; the seal hunt; and the western boat and Bank fisheries of the south coast.

For the purposes of this review it was found helpful to draw a distinction between "resident outport merchants" who lived the full range of their adult lives in rural Newfoundland and the "merchant gentry" whose outport residency was an episode in their business and family life which was otherwise substantially spent in the Old Country or in St. John's.

The resident group may be more worthy of consideration for the Province's commemoration program. Existing commemorations tend to favour the merchant gentry."

The very broad and geographically dispersed sample of merchants considered by Cuff in his paper excludes, for unknown reasons, all of those merchant families which formed and developed the communities of the Southern Shore[4] of Newfoundland and which are of interest to me, including the Carters, Windsors, Sweetlands and Morrys.

---

[4] For those not from Newfoundland, the term "Southern Shore" may be confusing. This is not the South Coast of Newfoundland but rather that part of the Avalon Peninsula south of St. John's, the capital. Nowadays it comprises the area more generally referred to in tourist brochures as the "Irish Loop", including the Atlantic coast of the Avalon Peninsula, St. Mary's Bay and the eastern part of Placentia Bay. Although the area was settled originally by fish merchants and their crews from the southwest of England – the so-called West Country - later Irish "boys" were conscripted to replace English fishermen when the wages offered no longer enticed them to undertake such arduous voyages. Before long, Irish fishermen and Irish merchants outnumbered their English counterparts on the Shore.

I hope that this narrative, which largely focusses on just one of this breed of the last of the West Country Merchants (while touching briefly on some others) may serve as a sort of window into the lives of all the scores of small to medium scale merchants in the many outports around this island and provide some insights into what motivated them to abandon their comfortable lives in England and come to this new and more austere challenging environment.

Before proceeding with our story, I must acknowledge those whose work on this subject preceded my own and without whose assistance this book could never have been written.

So many people have contributed to the material contents of this book that it is hardly possible to know where to start in thanking them all. And I am sure that I will inadvertently forget to mention at least one contributor, so I must offer my apologies in advance.

First, of course, I must acknowledge my predecessors in the research of the Morry family, my Aunt Jean Funkhouser (née Morry) and Dad Morry. Starting in the early 1960s, these two collaborated on the task of taking an oral family history, putting it on paper and verifying, correcting and adding to it. The effort continued single-handed by Aunt Jean after the death of Dad Morry in 1972 and until Aunt Jean's own death in 1996.

In the earliest days of this research, this two-person team was augmented with the skillful and keen assistance of Nimshi Cole Crewe, then an archivist with the Provincial Archives of Newfoundland in St. John's. Independently Nimshi had been working on a theory that the original founders of the settlement of Ferryland and surrounding areas, George Calvert (later Lord Baltimore) and David Kirke, had left descendants in the area, and he believed that the Morrys might well have been a part of that family tree. It was for this reason that he first contacted Dad Morry and Aunt Jean, and the ensuing collaboration was mutually beneficial.

After Aunt Jean's death, when I took on the task of carrying this effort forward, I was initially encouraged and assisted by my daughter Gillian, but she soon moved on to other passions and interests.

It was about this time that I discovered I had a cousin, albeit not a close cousin (4th cousin) named Enid O'Brien (née Stanford) who still lived in Newfoundland where the most important source information was found and, more importantly, who had independently been studying our common forbears for decades.

Along with my good fortune in finding Enid, I was soon to make the acquaintance of four others with an interest in the project who also lived in Newfoundland: Jean Carter Stirling, an expert on the Carter family of Ferryland, with whom the Morrys were related through many marital and business ties (Jean is my 5th cousin, once removed); Kevin Reddigan (not related), the foremost authority on the first families who settled Caplin Bay (Calvert), a select group which included the Morrys; Ida Michael (née White), a walking encyclopedia of information on the families of Ferryland, with a special interest in the Morry and Carter lines from which she descends (Ida is my 3rd cousin); and Steve Barnable who, though not related, was born in Ferryland and has a strong and abiding interest and an in-depth knowledge of the settlement of that part of Newfoundland. To all of these wonderful people, I owe a huge thank you for their continuing efforts and assistance.

Other family members too numerous to name have played an important role in transcribing old documents and collaborating in ferreting out facts from the many fictions in the family lore. But special thanks are owed to my cousins Karen Chapman (née Funkhouser), Aunt Jean's daughter who has carried on with her mother's work; Fredi Caines (née Mercer), who has been the custodian of many of the family heirlooms in the form of early documents and assisted me in deciphering them; the late Jamie Morry, who transcribed a number of Dad Morry's diaries, from which parts of the Morry family history could be extracted; and to my brother Glen Morry, who likewise translated Dad Morry's sometimes almost indecipherable handwriting into text from which the family history could be expanded.

At a greater distance, I was fortunate enough to be "found" by an expert amateur genealogist in England, the late Margaret Dickson (née Bilverstone), who was the wife of a 7th cousin, Ray Dickson, then living in Teignmouth, Devon. Together, Margaret and I were able to piece together and prove the relationship between Ray and I and, in so doing, to connect my immigrant ancestor, Matthew Morry, to cousins, uncles and aunts in the Dartmouth area who previously I could only suspect were related.

Archivists at the Centre for Newfoundland Studies (CNS), the associated Archives and Special Collections unit (ASC), and the Maritime History Archive (MHA), all at Memorial University of Newfoundland (MUN), and The Rooms (Provincial Archives Division) stood by to lend a hand in delving into the vast archival resources under their respective care. A note of special thanks is owed to Larry Dohey, Melanie Tucker and Greg Walsh at The Rooms, Bert Riggs and Joan Ritcey, now both retired and Patrick Warner and Colleen Quigley at the CNS, Linda White at the ASC, and Dave Bradley at the MHA. The late Dr. Keith Matthews at the MHA, whom I unfortunately never had the opportunity to meet before his death in 1984, was the source of the "Name Files" [5], from which so many clues on the Morry family history have been derived. Many others too numerous to name at these institutions as well as at the British National Archives in Kew, the Devon Archives in Exeter and Library and Archives Canada in Ottawa have lent a willing hand whenever required. I also engaged the services of a professional researcher, Susan T. Moore, who

---

[5] *Keith Matthews Name Files, 1500-1850*; [textual] 54 metres. Maritime History Archive, Memorial University of Newfoundland.

specialises in the court documents of the 16th to 19th centuries in England, to help me obtain some of the remaining court documents pertaining to my immigrant ancestor's numerous and not very illustrious appearances in the Court of King's Bench and High Court of Chancery.

After more than twenty years of work, the aggregate total of my efforts being put on paper, and wishing to obtain an unbiased opinion of its merits as a possible publication, I enlisted the editorial expertise of a very special friend and fellow writer, Larry Coady, former President of the Newfoundland and Labrador Historical Society. Larry was able to recognise very quickly that I was attempting to accomplish too much with the manuscript I presented him, encompassing parallel lines of study on genealogy, law and history. To him, I owe a special debt of gratitude for setting me back on track again, and this revised and more focussed manuscript exists largely because of his insight.

Finally, a note of special thanks goes to my dearest friend, my wife Jamie, whose years as a senior executive assistant in government came to the fore in performing the final detailed edits of the manuscript.

This has been a combined effort of all of the above and, though I may have done a great deal of the "grunt work" of data collection and compilation since 1996 at least, the lion's share of the credit for the final results goes to them. Where there are errors in the results, as inevitably there must be, it was my task alone to ferret them out and remove them, and I accept full responsibility for any oversights in so doing.

CHAPTER ONE - LAND AND SEA

John Morey was an angry man. The thing was, he didn't know with whom he should be most angry. He was angry at his grandfather, William, for coming to settle in this God-forsaken backwater, Stoke Gabriel. Wherever William came from, there must have been more opportunities there for a man with ambition to make his way in life. People talked about how lovely and quaint the village was. What matter did that make? It didn't put food on the table for his nine children (and a tenth on the way), or gold in his purse to buy a few of the better things in life. He was stuck here in the "Bishop's Peculiar", just like his father and grandfather before him. They might as well be serfs or indentured servants for the progress the family had made in three generations on the Bishop's land.

Figure 1. A View of Stoke Gabriel on the Dart River

He was mad at the Crown, or the Church; they were pretty much one and the same as far as he and every other ordinary worker were concerned. The only difference was that German George was on the throne in London and Stephen Weston, the new Bishop, was in Exeter. Being closer didn't make him any less of a tyrant; he was out for his own, just as that pirate, Lancelot Blackburne, who came before him, had been. Together they were responsible for what was in effect a feudal system that had long since outlived its time and that kept strong and able-bodied men like him from ever owning their own land and bettering themselves. He worked in the fields from sun up to sun down, every day of the week, save the Lord's Day, season in, season out. And the best he could expect at the end of the year, after paying the Bishop's land agent his share of the proceeds from the harvest, that is, if he was lucky and it had been a good year, was to be able to buy food and clothing for his family, and a shroud to bury them in when they died. They owned neither the house they lived in (a hovel, more like it), nor the farm implements with which he made his living, and certainly not the land on which he and his forefathers had slaved for three generations now.

But most of all, he had to admit, he was angry at himself. For if anything was to be done about it, only he could take the bull by the horns and do it. For the love and honour of Heaven! This was

1726, not the dark ages, and men should be able to do what it takes to help themselves and take control of their circumstances. He wasn't educated, but he could spell his name, more or less, though it sometimes came out as Morey, Mory or Moary; what odds, people knew who he was. He had no trade, unless you counted a strong back as a trade. But he wouldn't be the first Morey to strike out on his own to make his fortune. Wasn't there talk of his namesake, John Morry[6], admittedly only a second cousin or something, who had gone to sea, risen to the rank of Master and made a fortune as a privateer. He and his wife set themselves up in a fine house with a decent piece of land in the country and had another townhouse in London. If that John could do it, why not he?

That was it then. His mind was made up. He would tell Elizabeth this very evening when he came home to his meagre supper. But first, he had to talk again with Robert Holdsworth about the proposition that Robert had made to set him up in Dartmouth. The Holdsworth's practically owned Dartmouth. They had been the Governors of Dartmouth Castle and the Members of House of Commons from Devon for generations and held a balance of power in the business of the port with their rivals (some might say archenemies) the Searles. The fact that they also still retained a country home in Stoke Gabriel had made it possible for John to gradually ingratiate himself with Robert and to work his way around to seeking his assistance in coming to work for him in

---

[6] The National Archives (UK), file HCA 26/1/153; Letters of Marque - Commander: John Morry. Ship: Arcana. Burden: 247 tons. Crew: 160. This file indicates that in 1691 a John Morry was serving as a licensed Privateer and Master and Commander on a vessel equipped with 26 guns and 16 pederos. Elsewhere we learn of he and his wife acquiring properties in the country and in London. He may or may not have been related to this family; the link has not been established. But another John Morry, the son of Matthew Morry, the immigrant to Newfoundland, was indeed a licensed Privateer a century later.

Dartmouth. Obviously, Robert owed him nothing, and there were plenty of able-bodied men to employ on their vessels plying the Newfoundland trade. But for some reason, Robert seemed to have taken a liking to John, or possibly it was because he had an eye for Mary, John's eldest, and the best looking of his daughters. She was but fourteen years of age, but John had seen the way Robert smiled at her. Regardless, it was time to put talk into action.

The following week, John borrowed a wagon, piled it high with their few belongings and the wife and nine children, and set off on the highroad to Dartmouth, nine miles away by road along the River Dart, though it would be less than five by the river itself if he could have found a boat that he could afford to take them there.

Robert Holdsworth was as good as his word and had made arrangements for a tenement on the Ropewalk for John and the family. It was now April and the MARY was to sail for Newfoundland on the next tide and John was to be on it. He hadn't even bothered to inform Tolcher, the Bishop's agent, of his departure. What had he ever done for John and his family only make their life difficult? No doubt he would find some unfortunate soul to fill his shoes within the month. Looking back, he realised that they were right; it was a pretty little village they were leaving. But he had no regrets and great expectations for what the future held.

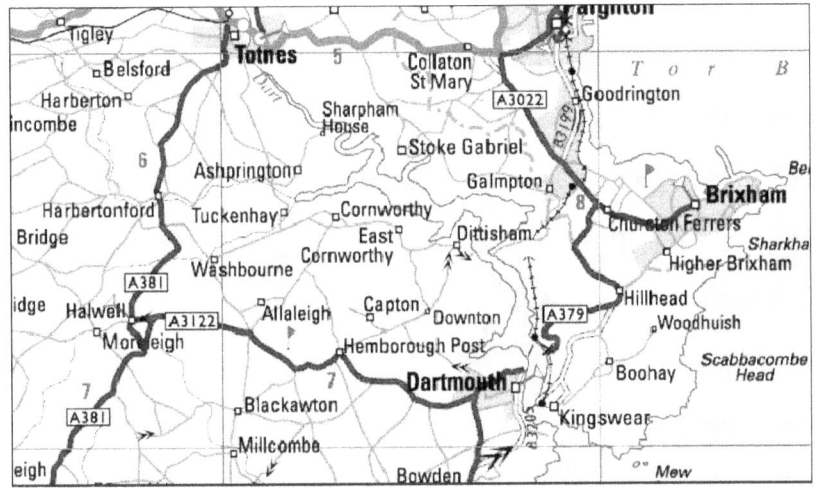

Figure 2. Stoke Gabriel, Dartmouth and the River Dart

CHAPTER TWO – BUILDING THE HISTORICAL NARRATIVE

The previous pages are fiction – or are they? The people mentioned existed; we know that. The John Morey mentioned was the grandfather of Matthew Morry, the shipowner and merchant who led his family to move from Dartmouth to the Southern Shore of Newfoundland in the late 1700s. What we do not know is much of anything about the lives of his predecessors, what they thought and what caused them to make certain life-altering decisions, like the reasons for John's grandfather William coming to Stoke Gabriel in 1650, or the move by John Morey and his family from Stoke Gabriel to Dartmouth that took place in or around 1726.

That is the trouble with attempting to build a complete, well-researched and factual family history. Prior to 1800, unless your family happens to have been royalty, or at least of the upper classes, the chances are pretty slim of finding sufficient details on their lives to flesh out a full account of your family history, without resorting to some speculation at least. In the case of my family, the Morry family of Caplin Bay (now Calvert) and Ferryland, Newfoundland, fortuitously they came from a part of England, the

South Hams District of Devon, specifically Dartmouth, and prior to that Stoke Gabriel, where church records existed going back into the 1500s in some churches. Also, fortuitously, they were practicing members of the "one true church" (Anglicans) and not Papists (Roman Catholics) or Dissenters (Methodists and allied breakaway Protestant faiths). In the case of religions other than the Church of England, scant records of baptisms, marriages and burials would have been kept. Census records in England were only kept in a consistent, national form beginning in 1851. There are some "census substitutes", such as records of payment of land taxes and tithes to churches, that are at least partially available for some communities. But once again, they apply primarily to those who owned land and those who could afford to support the church – possibly one percent of the population.

While these inherent stumbling blocks to historical research are an impediment to gaining a complete understanding of any given family's history, for the purposes of this book we are focussing on one member of the Morry family, Matthew Morry (1750-1836). He was the sole immigrant ancestor of all the Morrys who can trace their roots to Newfoundland. Fortunately for us, much more is known about him because of his appearance on Muster Rolls, his extensive business dealings, and, in particular, his many related legal challenges.

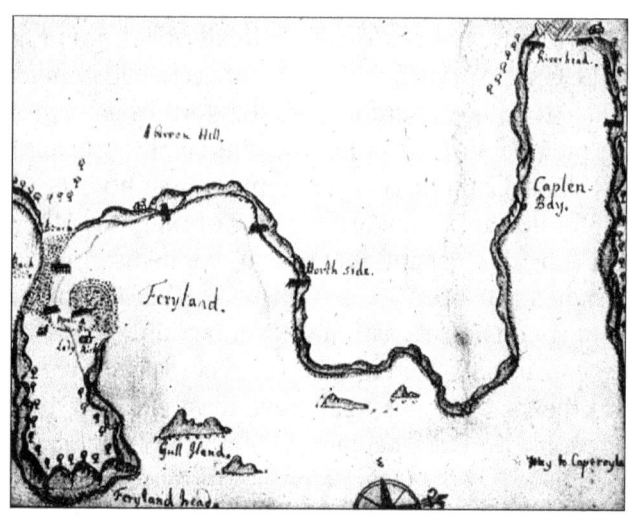

Figure 3. James Yonge Map of Ferryland and Caplin Bay, 1663[7]

Some Cautionary Notes

Before proceeding with the story of Matthew Morry and his kin prior to and after emigrating to Newfoundland, it is worthwhile to briefly mention a number of potential pitfalls that accompany the research undertaken to develop a full picture of this family.

Anyone involved in family history research will already know that you start with living family members and the information that they can provide first hand and then work your way backward

---

[7] The map above was drawn by James Yonge in 1663, almost one hundred years before Matthew Morry would have first set eyes on the place as a boy sailing on a fishing vessel from Dartmouth. James Yonge was shipped by his father as a surgeon on the REFORMATION. He recorded his observations of Newfoundland in a memoir more recently published in F.N.L. Poynter, ed., The Journal of James Yonge (1647-1721): Plymouth Surgeon; London: Longman, Green & Co. Ltd.; 1963.

using documentary sources held by the family. Of course, to quote a *bon mot* popular amongst such researchers, "oral history isn't worth the paper it is printed on". By that I mean, memory is a fragile recording mechanism that tends to get weaker with age. So, nothing you learn from a family member can be taken at face value without verification against a primary source. This is a lesson I learned from carefully examining, during the course of my research, the fondly held stories of our ancestors told to us by Dad Morry and previously told to him by earlier family members. Many "facts" about our ancestors turned out not to be facts at all.

But even written records such as those often found in family bibles, which are the much sought-after holy grail of family historians for the recorded life events they often contain from generations past, cannot always be taken on face value either.

Recently, I was thrilled to be given access to a massive old family bible that purported to contain correct names and dates of baptism, marriage and death on a family connected to my main line. I took photographs of the pages in this ancient book (said to be at least 160 years old and when I got home I began to look for what new gems I had discovered. When the first dates recorded proved to be at odds with the information I had previously recorded from church and government records I initially took this to be one more example of the kinds of inherent errors that exist in those types of information sources and so recorded the "new" information as the "preferred" data. I believed that family obtained information must invariably be better than any other kind. It did not take me long to realise, however, that virtually all the information in the old family bible was at odds with the "official" version of those dates. Consistent discrepancies of that kind cannot simply be pushed aside and ignored. I came to the conclusion, reluctantly, that the unknown person who, years ago, had recorded the information in the bible was not recording that information accurately. Perhaps he or she was relying too much on a failing memory or was suffering from Alzheimer's. Perhaps they had asked others to provide this information and never checked to see if the information they were being given was correct.

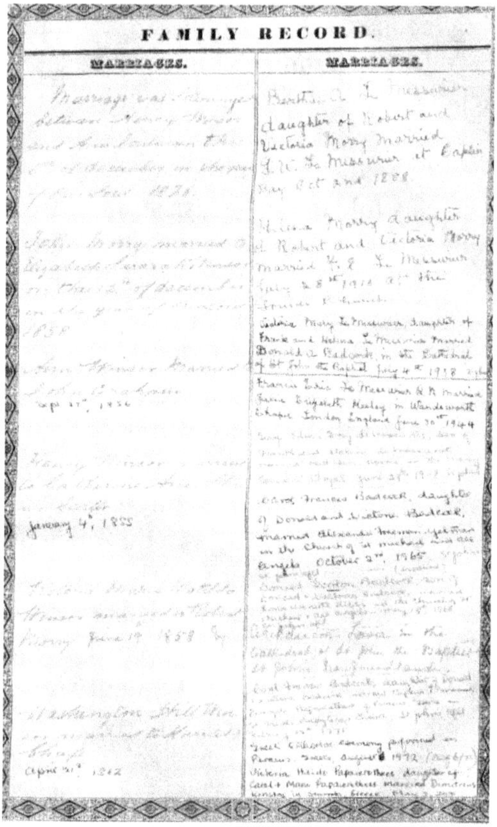

Figure 4. A Page from Ann Coulman's Bible

This is a valuable object lesson because, for all of these and many other reasons, personally obtained information based on interviews with family members is potentially prone to error and cannot be accepted on face value without verification. It's not only men who forget their wedding anniversaries, and even the most doting parent, especially late in life, may forget the exact dates of their children's birth, baptism and marriage. And one does not have to be a heartless child to forget the exact date of one's parents' or grandparents' deaths. These things happen. Recognizing this human failing, no family historian should ever accept information from a relative as 100% reliable until they themselves have verified it against an "official" source document. Fortunately, for recent generations at least, these are easily available from government offices for a small fee.

When living memory and records in family documents have been scoured for all the data that they can provide, it is then necessary to turn to what is known as "primary sources" for further information – such things as church registers and censuses for example. These are generally held to be the gold standard for historical research on families.

However, even here it must be remembered that original sources such as church registers contain information written down by a person who was not a member of the family and who may or may not have been present at the baptism, marriage or burial. In larger churches, the Minister or Priest who performed the ceremony quite often relied upon a curate, clerk or sexton to enter the record in the registry, sometimes days or weeks after the event. This invariably led to variations in the spelling of the name, as mentioned above, but also errors in the exact date that the ceremony took place. In England, a peculiarity of the system of record keeping in the Church of England was the requirement for the local minister to submit a copy of the entries in his register to the diocese in the form of what were referred to as Bishop's Transcripts. Regardless of whether the minister undertook this onerous and undoubtedly grudging task, or it was assigned to someone else in the church to undertake, every transcript of this kind is prone to human error. The tedium involved in preparing such a copy of hundreds of entries every year is largely responsible for such errors. That, and the fact that the handwriting in the original register would vary in legibility according to the handwriting skills of the person originally entering the information. Because of this, Bishop's Transcripts are never to be used as a primary source and should always be verified against the original register where possible. Unfortunately, in far more instances than one might imagine, the Bishops Transcript is all that remains of some church records due to the destruction of the original register when the church burned to the ground or when water or mould damage made the original register unreadable. Ironically, on the other hand, I have found a few instances in which a comparison of the original register and the Bishop's Transcript has shown that this second "kick at the can" gave the recorder the opportunity to correct or render more complete the entry originally made in the register. Thus, where possible, it is always wise to compare entries in both sources and record any differences found, along with an analysis of the potential reasons for the differences and an assessment of their respective credibility.

In Newfoundland, there were no Bishop's Transcripts. However, there was a unique situation which developed with regard to duplication of entries in the registers of St. Thomas's (the Garrison Church) and the Anglican Cathedral of St. John the Baptist in the mid-1800s. This occurred during the period between when the fifth of the original wooden Churches that stood in this location was destroyed by fire (during the Great Fire of 1846) and the time when the new stone Cathedral was formally consecrated (ca 1850) and it seems for years after that, since the process of rebuilding the Cathedral went on for a very long time after its re-consecration. In that period, St. Thomas's, which survived all the great fires of St. John's unscathed, served as the *de facto* seat for the Bishop (his so-called "Cathedral Church"). Consequently, when looking for the record of an ancestor and finding it in the Cathedral register, it is always wise to check the St. Thomas's register for the same event. In many instances it will be found there as well and, in fact, for exactness in your record, you should be able to determine if the ceremony physically took place at St.

Thomas's or at the Cathedral itself, depending on the year that the event occurred. Many discrepancies can be found in the recording of information on the same event in these two registers so caution must be observed.

The same would also be true for a period of time after the present stone Cathedral was largely destroyed in the Great Fire on July 8, 1892, until it was partially rebuilt in 1895 and finally rededicated in 1905. However, by then, civil Vital Records were being kept and there was, therefore, an alternative relatively reliable source of information of this kind.

Cathedral Ruins After the Great Fire of 1892

Figure 5. Anglican Cathedral and St. Thomas's ca 1892

Government records are another major source of information for family historians. But here too there are precautions that must be observed. I won't go into detail but suffice to say that census information and vital statistics transcripts of church registers are as prone to error as the sources mentioned above for much the same reasons.

Another problem area is the physical quality of original source records, especially those few that date back to the pre-1800 era. In many cases, those original sources have suffered from various climatic and environmental conditions that have led to their deterioration, to a greater or lesser extent, resulting in the legibility of the records being impaired. In the course of my research, I have occasionally come across an original church register hundreds of years old that is in pristine condition and in which the handwriting in which the records were laid down is a joy to read. I celebrate such moments, because they may never occur again during the course of my research.

Generally speaking, records that are permitted to be publicly examined at archives in London (the National Archives at Kew) and in St. John's (the Provincial Archives Division of The Rooms) are very frail, often faded or water damaged, and sometimes crumble to the touch. For this reason, more and more of these original records are being taken out of circulation for conservation and preservation. While some may gradually be made available for public examination, once stabilized to prevent further deterioration, even in the limited amount of time I have been conducting research on such documents it has become less and less common to be granted actual access to such original documents and, before long, it will probably be impossible, except in the case of academics with strong and compelling reasons for needing to examine the originals for their research purposes.

Recently, on a research trip to the British National Archives, I sought to examine the Port Books for Dartmouth from the late 1700s to study the involvement of my immigrant ancestor, Matthew Morry's company (called somewhat unimaginatively Matthew Morry and Company) in the Newfoundland Trade. I was shocked to discover that these books, which were prepared on very low-quality paper something like newsprint, were still available for examination. I felt guilty handling these precious old records because I knew that each page I touched crumbled a little and that it would not take many more examinations by other researchers before the information contained on these pages would be lost to history forever. But even a well-endowed institution like the National Archives does not have resources sufficient to preserve and/or digitise or film all of the documents in their collection. Less so the Provincial Archives in Newfoundland, where they currently lack dedicated and trained conservation specialists on staff.

So, it should not be surprising, and indeed should be lauded, when you inquire about the availability of a certain old record and are told that it is no longer available for public examination because of concerns for its conservation. Only, hopefully, before such a decision has to be taken, a reasonable copy in some form should be made to provide a decent second-best alternative that those who are interested can consult.

The Path Ahead

This book will follow the trail of the Morry family only. There are enough rogues, heroes and incredible personages in that one line to provide the fodder for one book and more without any difficulty. Moreover, the challenges encountered in researching this line will present the reader with most of the problems and hurdles they too will face when following their own family lines back through the mists of time. Matthew Morry (the first of the name), who was the immigrant ancestor and patriarch of the Morry line in Newfoundland, represents what I believe to be a prime example of the kind of small-scale merchant whose unsung efforts kept the outport communities of Newfoundland struggling along through good times and bad while Newfoundland grew from an exclusive fishing station of the wealthy West Country Merchants to a self-governing colony, and later a Dominion in the British Empire.

Figure 6. An Exeter-Dartmouth Port Book from 1710

CHAPTER THREE – EARLY ROOTS IN STOKE GABRIEL

The Earliest Known Members of Matthew Morry's Family

Before we can even begin to describe the role that a family like the Morrys played in the early development of their small chosen part of Newfoundland we need to understand a bit more about the family itself and its roots in Devon.

So, what do we know about the Morrys of Devon and how do we know it? To start with, let us set aside all concerns for the spelling of that surname. As in the case of John Morey mentioned above, a factual individual in a possibly fictitious scenario, almost none of the working class prior to 1800 was educated enough to be able to read and write. Some could spell their name, but like John, their writing and spelling were so elementary and illegible that their names, when they wrote them, often came out in a variety of forms. Those who could not write their own name were entirely at the mercy of the clerics who recorded those names in church registers and the government or business figures who recorded them for their purposes (recording debts, legal disputes, taxes owing, etc.). Hence, in the case of Morry, a spelling that only came into vogue in Dartmouth in the late 1700s, and was in more consistent use in Newfoundland after 1800, the name appears in at least these forms in documents that I believe pertain to my line: Mory, Moary, Morey, Morrye, Morye, Mawry, Mourye, Moore. The late Geoffrey Williams of New Zealand, who was the acknowledged world leader of research on the "single name study" of the name Morey and its variants, contended that there were over two dozen spellings of the name that were all associated with the same stock over the very long term. He also believed that the name may have had Moorish roots because his theory was that the Moreys of southern England were descendants of North African stock via the Moorish invasion of Spain and the Balearic Islands. No one really put much stock in that theory except Geoffrey.

But interestingly, in a book entitled *"Early-Stuart Mariners and Shipping 1619-1635"* by Dr. Todd Gray (see References), a well-known researcher in Devon, several mariners from that era bear names that are remarkably familiar. For example, Mathew Morishe and Mathew Morice of St. Minver, most likely the same person, but also Richard Morishe of Padstow, Robert Morhay of Lympstone, Michael Morrye of Kingsteignton, Stephen Morrys of Kingswear, Leonard and William Morrice of Dittisham and Hughe Moorishe of St. Ewe. Any or all of these men may have been ancestors of the Morry line. All of these little communities are close by both Stoke Gabriel and Dartmouth.

In fact, no consistency in the spelling of the name in my line occurred until they left behind the Tower of Babel that was England and arrived in Newfoundland. In Newfoundland only two spellings of the name existed, Morey and Morry, and it seems likely that the spelling Morry was chosen by my immigrant ancestor, Matthew Morry, and his family to distinguish between them and a clan of Irish Roman Catholics who went by the name Morey and who arrived in Newfoundland directly from Ireland, by coincidence, at about the same time.

As mentioned above, I was fortunate enough to be gifted with a partially researched family tree when I began my studies twenty years ago or so. In my case, my late Aunt Jean [Morry] Funkhouser picked up the torch at the behest of her father, Howard Leopold Morry, in the early 1960s. "Dad Morry" was an amateur historian of great renown, the keeper of the family lore, a fabulous raconteur, and a prodigious diarist who recorded in writing many times over his recollections of the old stories passed down from generation to generation. In those days, of course, there were no computers and no "online resources" to turn to.

This was even prior to the Church of the Latter-Day Saints (Mormon), often abbreviated as LDS, microfilming of English church records in the 1970s, an enormous boon to researchers, saving much travel, time and money. Research in those days meant either hiring a local researcher, an expensive proposition, or travelling in person to the location where paper records are preserved. Sometimes this also entailed having to plead with the clergy or custodians to have access to the records they jealously guarded before poring over those records for days or weeks, once access had been accorded, in search of relevant facts.

This was, in fact, the method followed by Dr. Keith Matthews, one of the foremost authorities on the early settlement and fisheries of Newfoundland. To quote the Maritime History Archive's introduction to his collected works:

> *Dr. Keith Matthews, a founding member and former chair of the Maritime History Group, during his tenure at Memorial, amassed and created a huge collection of documents and papers relating the early fisheries and settlement of Newfoundland and the individuals who were involved in its economic and political life. The basis of the collection was data*

assembled during research for his doctoral thesis on the Newfoundland/West of England fisheries, and later research projects.

In carrying out their preliminary research, Aunt Jean and Dad Morry had an ally in the form of Nimshi Cole Crewe. Nimshi had been an accountant with the Revenue Department of the Newfoundland Government during the Commission of Government days before Confederation with Canada (when Canada joined Newfoundland, as we Newfoundlanders like to say). After Confederation, with the changeover of administration in matters related to federal and provincial responsibilities, many former employees of the "national" government of Newfoundland found themselves at loose ends initially, and Nimshi was amongst them. But he soon found his feet again as an archivist with the newly established Provincial Archives of Newfoundland, even though he had no technical training in that area. In the early 1960s, Nimshi became convinced that there were descendants of George Calvert, later Lord Baltimore, the founder of the Colony of Avalon (now Ferryland) and his successor, David Kirke, still living in Newfoundland. As part of his research into that theory, he came to know Dad Morry. Dad Morry was well known in Ferryland and the surrounding area of the Southern Shore as a local historian with a prodigious memory and an encyclopedic knowledge of the old lore. More than that, he was also a descendant of the original Robert Carter, the defender of Ferryland, whom Nimshi believed was connected in some way to the Baltimore/Kirke line. Nimshi's theory was eventually disproven, much to his regret, but the collaboration between him and Dad Morry on this and other topics of mutual interest in relation to Newfoundland history only grew. Through their association, and in frequent correspondence with Aunt Jean in Utah, the first family tree of the Morrys began to take shape.

It may or may not be true, but family lore has it that Aunt Jean actually became a Mormon partly in order to have access to the colossal repository of family records that the church maintains in the Granite Mountain Records Facility in Salt Lake City, Utah. True or not, we know that she did convert and it is an incontestable truth that, having done so, her research was made that much easier and gained much more credibility and reliability through the training she thereby received.

By the time that I received a mimeographed copy of the Pedigree Charts and Family Group Sheets that she had compiled from information obtained from family members as well as personal and contracted research, sometime in 1996, the year she passed away, it appeared that Aunt Jean had managed to follow both her paternal and maternal lines back five or six generations prior to their emigration to Newfoundland. She had used both LDS resources in Utah and the assistance of paid researchers in Britain, but in neither case was this information vetted against original sources by her or anyone else. Even so, these research results had then been submitted to and accepted by the LDS International Genealogical Index (IGI)[8] and were now in the public domain. Despite the deficiencies, this was an excellent start for the times.

---

[8] A database of several hundred million entries compiled from submissions by Church members and later volunteers. It was compiled from its inception in 1973 until it was replaced by more comprehensive and better vetted information in the form of the Ancestral File and more recently the Pedigree Resource File on the current website, FamilySearch. Amongst its many deficiencies, the IGI notably contained no information on burials. Also, and this is a deficiency of its successor services, the Ancestral File, Pedigree Resource File and much of what is found on the FamilySearch website, this is secondary data provided by contributors and hence prone to human error. Only the data derived from the LDS's own volunteer-based transcribing projects is vetted for accuracy by more knowledgeable and experienced referees.

Many amateur genealogists are satisfied with such a bare-bones family tree. In Aunt Jean's case, it gave her sufficient information on her direct ancestors to fulfil her religious duties, which for Mormon's entails the posthumous baptism of ancestors so that they may be counted amongst the saved. For others, their only real interest is to know from whom they descended, and anything pertaining to siblings and spouses is of no interest to them. But for people with a broader historical bent like me, that is completely unacceptable. I wanted to know everything there was to know about everyone even remotely connected to my ancestors. This set me off on a path that has led to, among other results, a family tree to over 25,000 individuals. This may seem to some excessive, but in a small and, until very recently, remote and cut-off part of Newfoundland like the Ferryland area, it makes a fascinating study in and of itself to follow the dynamics of intermarriage amongst the few families that have settled and remained there for hundreds of years. And inevitably this acquired knowledge contributed greatly to an understanding of the class dynamics and the societal interplay that form such a rich part of the history of this and any similar remote region of Newfoundland.

A snapshot view of the generations in the Morry family leading back from myself is found in Appendix 1. It consists of five generations of Newfoundland births preceded by six generations of births in Devon, the first being the William Mory mentioned in Chapter One - Land and Sea.

Stoke Gabriel in the 16th and 17th Centuries

So, let us return then, to the earliest roots of the Morry family in Devon, which are supported by solid evidence, and make from those facts what we can with only a little supposition to fill in the missing details. First of all, the place where William Mory chose for unknown reasons, to move, marry and raise his family.

If you are an anglophile, as I have become during the course of studying my family history, and if you have in mind a sort of Aristotelian image of the quintessential English country village, that image would be Stoke Gabriel. In fact, it is such a prototype of such villages that it was used as the template for the fictional village of Thornford Regis in the crime novels of C. C. Benison. I've included a few photographs of the village here but, honestly, photographs cannot do it justice. It is just too "picture perfect"!

Figure 7. Stoke Gabriel from Cornworthy across the River Dart

Figure 8. St. Gabriel Churchyard, the River Dart Estuary

The history of Stoke Gabriel as a settlement is ancient. According to Ray Freeman in *Dartmouth and its Neighbours*, the village existed in Roman times.

Once the Romans withdrew, the Celtic farmers endured repeated invasions by the Saxons, the Danes (Vikings) and the Normans in turn. When the Domesday book was produced in 1086, the area around Stoke Gabriel fell under the protection of the Bishop of Exeter, and so it remained right up to the time that William Morry first appeared in the village six hundred years later. The existing church of St. Gabriel, or at least parts of it, and the ancient yew in the churchyard are believed to pre-date the Domesday book.

Despite its obvious appeal as a bucolic and beautiful country village along the River Dart, the fact remains that, in earlier days, it would have not have been ideally placed if one was involved in the marine trades. Stoke Gabriel is approximately five miles (eight kilometres) by water up the River Dart from Dartmouth[9] and would have been above the comfort level of accessible navigation (the river is prone to siltation and has always required constant dredging to maintain navigation) by larger ocean-going sailing ships during the days of the Newfoundland codfish trade. Aside from which, all the ships' chandlers and purveyors of necessities for the trade were located in Dartmouth, which was located at the mouth of the River Dart, as its name so abundantly makes clear. So, the obvious question that comes to mind is, were the Moreys, during their three generations spent in Stoke Gabriel, mariners, as were all of the later family members, or were they then employed, as my speculative former chapter suggested, as farm labourers or tenant farmers?

The economy of Stoke Gabriel in the 16th and 17th centuries largely revolved around the obviously verdant and productive surrounding countryside and not the more distant sea. Note, however, that this is not a universal truth. Historically, it is believed that the once plentiful salmon run and bass fishery on the Dart River, as well as a rich but not as lucrative crab harvest, were what attracted people to settle in this area as long as one thousand years ago. The bass fishery is all but gone but the salmon and crab fisheries continue to this day, though the salmon resource is now much depleted as well.

Also, Stoke Gabriel was the site of the country homes of a number of famous figures associated with maritime activities including the explorer John Davis, after whom the Davis Strait in the Canadian Arctic is now named.

Ray Freeman, in her book, *Dartmouth and its Neighbours*, goes on to tell us that:

---

[9] See Figure 3. Stoke Gabriel, Dartmouth and the River Dart, South Hams

"In the 16th century, John Davis the navigator was born at Sandridge and grew up to be a friend of the Gilbert family in Greenway. Sandridge manor was by then owned by the Pomeroy family, and Davis probably lived in the barton [literally a barnyard, but here she means a farm building]."

Later, she tells us:

"Sandridge was bought by Lord Ashburton. A. W. O. Holdsworth[10] and Henry Hunt both lived at Maisonette at different times, and Sir R. L. Newman also had property there."

These three gentlemen were all major merchants in both Dartmouth and Newfoundland.

Figure 9. Sandridge Estate, Stoke Gabriel

---

[10] Arthur William Olive Holdsworth, from whom Matthew Morry's grandson, John Henry Morry, and his business partner, Peter Paint Le Messurier, would purchase the Holdsworth estate and fishing room in Ferryland in 1844.

Figure 10. The John Davis Monument in Dartmouth

Arthur Holdsworth, the governor of Dartmouth Castle, a onetime Fishing Admiral of St. John's in the late 17th and early 18th Centuries, and a leader in the development of the cod fishery in Newfoundland at the end of the 1600s also had a country home near Stoke Gabriel. His family conducted business in Ferryland and in St. John's until the early 1800s when their interests were bought out in part by my 2nd great grandfather, John Henry Morry, and his brother-in-law and partner, Peter Paint Le Messurier (more on this relationship later).

Figure 11. John H. Morry and Holdsworth House, ca 1890

The Hunt family, which was long associated with the Newman family in their fisheries-related business enterprises in Newfoundland, still maintains a country home in Stoke Gabriel.

Sir Humphrey Gilbert, who claimed Newfoundland in the name of her majesty, Queen Elizabeth I, on August 5, 1583, as well as his half-brothers, Sir Walter Raleigh and Carew Raleigh, grew up in Compton, only a few miles from Stoke Gabriel. Although Compton Castle was the family seat, Gilbert was actually born in Greenway, a country home even closer to Stoke Gabriel near Galmpton. Greenway is now better known as the home of Agatha Christie and is where she wrote all of her novels. On a visit to Greenway today, there is never a mention of the connection to Gilbert and Newfoundland. But when one visits Compton Castle, as I did in April 2017, and if one is lucky enough, as I was, to have a guided tour by the current owners, Geoffrey and Angela Gilbert, the whole story is laid out for you. As Geoffrey Gilbert succinctly and aptly tells us in the introduction to the guidebook to Compton Castle:

> *Historically, my family's greatest claim to fame is its involvement in the early attempts to colonise the New World. Sir Humphrey Gilbert's colonisation of Newfoundland in 1583 founded the British Empire. He was followed by his half-brother, Sir Walter Raleigh, who took up the challenge and organised the Roanoke colony on the Outer Banks of North Carolina in 1585. Sir Humphrey's son Raleigh Gilbert sailed to what is now Maine and set up Fort St George in 1607.*

Figure 12. Sir Humphrey Gilbert Monument in Dartmouth

But all of these famous mariners and adventurers called the area their country home, while their exploits on the sea were not conducted from this location, which is so remote from the sea proper.

All that said and done, historically, as recently as 1831, when the first census was carried out, virtually every person declared as employed in Stoke Gabriel was in one way or another associated with the agriculture industry, and it is safe to assume that this statistic had not changed much over the years from the days of the earliest Morry presence in the parish.

So, again, the question must be asked, what brought them to the village in the early 1600s? And the simple answer is, we don't know! Neither the marriage record of William Mory and Jennet Full in 1650 nor the birth/baptismal records of their 12 children over the next two decades give any clue as to the occupation of the father. Regrettably, as excellent as the church register records are for Stoke Gabriel, it was not the practice of the ministers of those days to record a father's or husband's occupation, as it often was in other parishes and at other times. We can deduce that he was not a man of means because he did not own land. That would be a matter of public record for taxation purposes. It is also likely, for the same reason, that he did not own the house or houses in which they lived, because there are no records of such ownership. But again, we must not be too hasty to leap to such conclusions because a lack of evidence should never be used as evidence to prove a theory.

William Mory (ca 1624-1692)

8th Great Grandfather

So, let's start with what we do know. The marriage record for William Mory and Jennet Full appears in the St. Gabriel parish register on Sept. 23, 1650. The original register was remarkably well preserved when it was microfilmed for posterity for the South West Heritage Trust and Parochial Church Council and the pages are all available for download (for the price of membership) from the Find My Past website (http://www.findmypast.com).

For William and his family, the register at St. Gabriel also provides the records of birth/baptism of all of their children (at least we assume that these are all their children; stillbirths and some early infant mortalities are not always recorded in church registers). See Appendix 2 for a summary of his family.

These are pretty impressive results for a family that existed three hundred and fifty years ago! Not many researchers are lucky enough to have this much information on their subjects from this era. That said, we still are no further ahead in determining where and when William was born and why he chose to move to Stoke Gabriel.

I will not go into the details of all the possibilities I have examined for the birthplace and parentage of William. Suffice to say that there is no definitive answer to these questions at this time and hence, in genealogical terms, William is the "brick wall" in our research.

John Mory (1663-1736)

7th Great Grandfather

Having exhausted all avenues of research to move back the curtains of time hiding the Morry ancestry prior to William Mory of Stoke Gabriel, we will now turn to what we know and what we do not know about his successors in the family line.

The first of these is his son, John Mory, whose Christening record is found in the Stoke Gabriel register on January 1, 1663, and reads:

"[1662] 1 Jan. John filia Will$^{m.}$ Mory & Jennet ux."

The partial use of Latin ("filia" = son; "ux.", short for "uxor" = wife) in this register seems to imply that the church was still in transition from the old RC nomenclature, no longer in vogue in most Church of England registers.

So at least we have a solid baptism or Christening record for John, unlike his father, though we do not know for certain his actual date of birth. It is normal to assume in such cases that the birth occurred shortly prior to the Christening, except in coastal parishes where it was often the case that a child was born during the absence of one or both parents from the parish and not Christened until they were all present once again. So, for simplicity sake, we will give him a birth year of 1663[11].

---

[11] In the old calendar January 1, 1662 would be 1663 today.

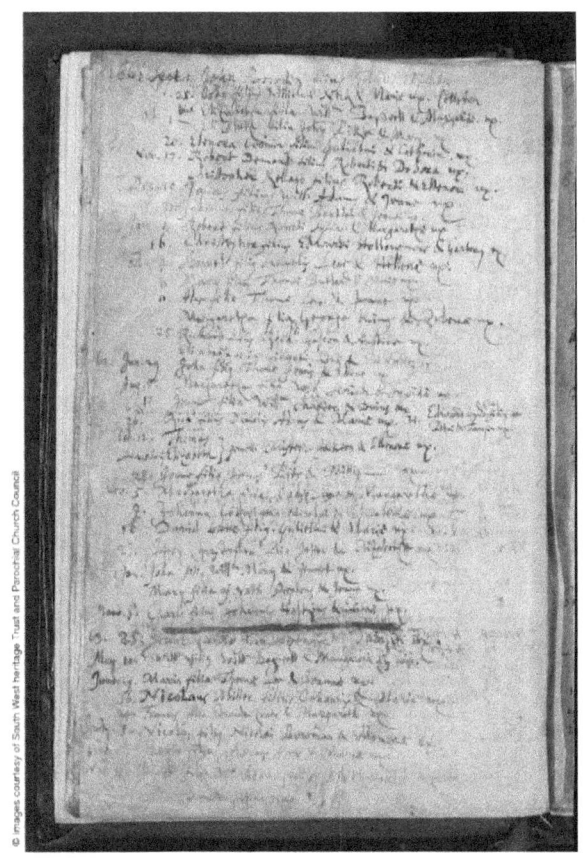

Figure 13. Baptismal Record of John Mory (1663-1736)

Unfortunately, unlike his father, we do not have a burial record for John, though we know he died before his wife Susana, because she was noted to be his widow at the time of her burial on February 23, 1736. But also, unlike his parents, we do not know the surname of his wife. There is no marriage record in the church register, and her surname does not appear on any of the baptism records of their children, nor even on her own burial record. The latter is no surprise because in the England of the day women lost their personal identity and became essentially an adjunct to their husband after marriage. The absence of the mother's surname on children's baptismal records of that era in England is also not surprising, unlike in Ireland, where this was almost always included, at least in Roman Catholic records, though probably not in Church of Ireland records. But the complete absence of so many records pertaining to John and Susanna is perplexing.

These missing entries bring up an interesting possibility, however. The Stoke Gabriel records are clear and, it would have appeared, comprehensive during these years. If there is no marriage record for this couple, they were likely married elsewhere. And if there was no record of John's burial in the parish, it is a pretty sure bet that he was not buried there. The most likely reason for the absence of these two records is that they were absent from the parish when the marriage took place and that he was elsewhere when he died. One of the most common reasons for a man not being buried in his home parish in those days would have been that he had been lost at sea. And if he was a mariner, at least if he was a ship's Master, in many cases they married elsewhere and brought home their spouse on their return voyage. Of course, there is no solid evidence of this, with one slight possibility.

A new contact, Gail McConnell of the Dartmouth History Research Group, put me onto the fact that there is a website called British History Online. There she found a reference to a minor appointment as Tidesman and Boatsman (that is, a local Customs Officer) in 1745 in Dartmouth that was granted to a John Morey who was either Matthew Morry's father or grandfather (both were of an age where it was possible that this referred to him). The date was well beyond when we know that the John Mory we are now discussing (Matthew's great grandfather) had gone to his reward. But while investigating this item on the website, I decided to do a generic search within the records held there on the surname Morey and came up with another reference to a John Morey, Esquire who was to be appointed captain-lieutenant under the reign of Mary and William in 1694. This was too early to have been Matthew's father or grandfather but it is entirely possible that this man is "our" current John Mory. Of course, there are other possibilities, and it cannot be stated for certain that this is the man, but pending further proof, I am tentatively laying claim to this distinction. Here is the reference to that find:

> *William and Mary: February 1694*
> *Pages 16-46*
> *Calendar of State Papers Domestic: William and Mary, 1694-5 </cal-state-papers/domestic/will-mary/1694-5>. Originally published by His Majesty's Stationery Office, London, 1906.*
> **Lumley's regiment; for John Morey, esquire, to be captain-lieutenant**
> *This premium content was digitised by double rekeying </about>. All rights reserved*
> *'William and Mary: February 1694', in Calendar of State Papers Domestic: William and Mary, 1694-5, ed. William John Hardy (London, 1906), pp. 16-46 http://www.british-history.ac.uk/cal-state-papers/domestic/will-mary/1694-5/pp16-46 [accessed 3 December 2015].*

The Family Group Sheet for John Mory and his wife Susanna is found in Appendix 2. What stands out most notably in this report is the fact that, not only are there significant gaps in the records for John and Susanna, but also gaps exist for most of their children, either a baptism record or a burial record, and quite likely missing marriage records for some where none is shown but where a marriage may actually have occurred. Thus, we have to conclude that the Stoke Gabriel register was not as inclusive as it would have at first appeared. The names of the children were those found in the IGI reports of Aunt Jean and those reports did not give any indication of how she became convinced that these children were indeed a part of this family if no baptism record existed. It seems hard to credit that, even with the vast resources of the LDS at her disposal, she could have accessed records in the mid-1960s that are not available through the power of the internet.

However, at one time there was an online parish clerk for Stoke Gabriel whose name was David Tolcher, and I was able to consult with him and have him conduct actual searches of the original register, which is still at St. Gabriel's church in Stoke Gabriel. Between us, we concluded that Aunt Jean's list of children was more than likely correct, though how she determined it is not known. Further evidence probably exists in her personal notes now in the possession of her daughter Karen.

Finally, of note is the occurrence of the name George in this family. It is not a carry-over from the family of William Mory and the possibility exists that it is, therefore, a name in use in the family of Jennet Full, though it does not appear to be that of her father or brothers that we know of. The name lingered in the Morey line and indeed did carry down through the line of Matthew Morry, the immigrant to Newfoundland. It was also in common use amongst his more distant cousins in Dartmouth, some of whom were Masters of vessels plying the Newfoundland trade, as he was at one time. More on this later.

CHAPTER FOUR - THE TRANSITION YEARS

Moving Back and Forth Between Stoke Gabriel and Dartmouth

John Morey (1687-1772)

6th Great Grandfather

Before moving on to a discussion of the next generation of the immediate ancestors of Matthew Morry, that of John Morey and his two wives, Elizabeth Stone and Elizabeth Matthews and their children, it is worth noting that John's brother, William, was the only other member of the Stoke Gabriel clan to move to Dartmouth. It is noted on his burial record in the register of St. Gabriel church that he was "of Dartmouth but buried here". The practice of returning the bodies of family members who died in Dartmouth for burial in Stoke Gabriel continued in John's family, with his first wife, Elizabeth Stone, and his son, William, and daughter, Joan, being buried in the St. Gabriel churchyard. Thus, this generation was truly a transitional one between the two places.

The English did not adhere rigidly to the naming tradition for children that was sacrosanct in Ireland. Here is an abridged version of a discussion of this subject by Fiona Fitzsimmons, found on the FindMyPast website:

> *In that tradition, the eldest son would be named after his paternal grandfather, the second son after his maternal grandfather, the third son after his father. It goes on from there, but this is sufficient for the current discussion. A similar pattern existed for naming the oldest daughters in a family. It was not as strictly adhered to, however, and frequently, amongst the wealthy at least, we see girl's names influenced by fashion. Unusually, this naming pattern for the sons was adhered to by all economic classes and across all denominations in Ireland. Consequently, it's not unusual to see the same names recurring within the family across generations. This can prove extremely helpful in linking names in your family tree together, particularly if the name in question is in any way unusual.*

In England, while the rigid pattern described above was not reliably followed, it was not uncommon for the first-born son to take his father's name (not his paternal grandfather's).

In the Morry clan, the first-born son of William Mory and Jennet Full was named William. Their second born was John, whose family was discussed in the previous section. Could it be that this meant William's father was named John? It is worth considering for future research.

In the family of John Mory and his wife Susana, their first-born son was named John, seemingly following the same pattern set in the previous generation. But the second son named George, a name that did not occur in the previous generation. That is unless another son was born and given that name but died at birth, therefore not being christened.

Three sisters preceded John, but oddly, it was the second of these three who was named after her mother, Susanna. The first was named after her paternal grandmother Gennet (or Jennet) Full. If that was indeed a pattern of naming being followed in the family, then there probably was a William who was born after John but who was either stillborn or who died so soon after birth that he could not be baptised and recorded in the church register. A gap of well over a year between the births of John and George suggests a possible missing child. Interestingly, it was the last of the known seven children born to John and Susanna who was named William, perhaps a second boy of the name, honouring the first who died.

John Morey J$^{r.}$ (this was the most commonly seen spelling of his surname) was married twice. First, he married Elizabeth Stone, by whom he had a first-born son named John, a second born son named William, and seven girls and two other boys before she died at age 47 in 1729. This was commonly the natural age of women in those days in England and there is no need to speculate on an unusual cause of death. They had been married nineteen years and yet had eleven children that we know of during that time. But at age 47, one would think that childbirth would be highly unlikely to have been the cause of her death. Yet the records appear to show that she did have a daughter in that year.

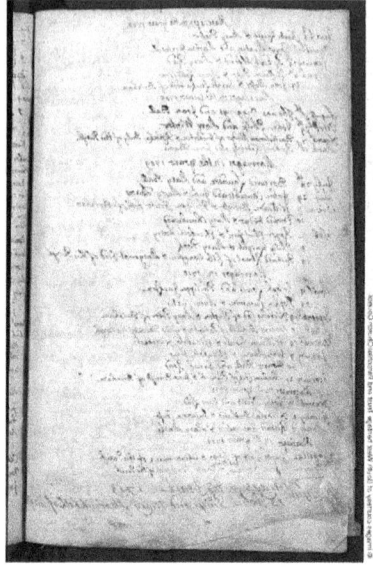 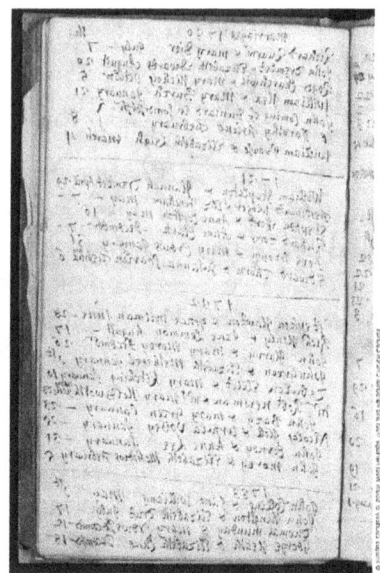

Figure 14. The Two Marriages of John Moury/Morey

In regard to John's second wife, Elizabeth Matthews, we find that in addition to the twelve children born to him by his first wife Elizabeth Stone, the second marriage yielded three more girls; Sarah, Joan and Mary. This second wife was much younger than the first and indeed much younger than John (she was born in Dartmouth in 1697), but oddly she does not appear to have been married previously, even though she was thirty-five when she married John. That would be unusual for the day. It also partly explains why they had only three children together, the final being born when she was forty-five. There is some doubt as to when she died. There is a burial record at St. Clement Townstal for Elizabeth Morey on the 14th of March 1763. However, there are no notations such as "wife of John". That was customary in the case of a married woman. It may simply have been an oversight on the part of the minister who recorded the burial.

An interesting fact about the children of John and his first wife, Elizabeth Stone, is that their youngest son was named Mathew. This name, which has been repeated in the family from that day to this, a period of almost three hundred years, at least once in every generation, never before existed in the Morey line. This leads me to suspect that there was a Mathew in Elizabeth's family, possibly even her father, whose name we do not know.

The name of their third son, Richard, also came into the family with this marriage. And it too was found in future generations. But it did not follow the line of Matthew Morry, our immigrant ancestor, any more than did George, rather becoming the forename of his cousins and following their lines of descendants. This included Capt. Richard Morrey, mentioned in a subsequent chapter, who served as Master of the DORSETSHIRE, owned by Matthew Morry and his partner, Walter Prideaux, at the time that she was taken as a prize by a French privateer in 1804, and then retaken by a Royal Navy vessel, leading to one of many court cases in which Matthew became embroiled during his career.

This John is one of two (the other being his son) who may have been the John Morey appointed as a Tidesman and Boatsman in Dartmouth in 1744 according to "British History Online". I think it most likely that it was not this man but rather his son, though it is impossible to be sure. This John would have been advanced in years at the time (70) and the job would require someone physically fit for such work. His son, John, was then in the prime of his working life at 33. In the absence of this appointment then, we have no idea what occupation John Sr. pursued that brought him to Dartmouth. But we can assume it was in some way connected to the Maritime industries, which employed virtually everyone but the shopkeepers and gentry in Dartmouth in those days.

Finally, a prime example of the variability of the spelling of surnames in these days can be seen in the naming of the father in this family. He was baptised as John Mory, married to his first wife as John Moury, married to his second wife as John Morey and finally buried as John Morey! As intimated above, it is vital that one be flexible in examining various spellings of surnames in searching for historical figures in the 18th century and earlier.

The Family Group Sheets of John Mory/Moury/Morey by his two wives are found in Appendix 2.

CHAPTER FIVE - THE DARTMOUTH-NEWFOUNDLAND CONNECTION

Dartmouth's Past

Dartmouth's position at the mouth of the Dart River virtually ensured that it would be occupied and exploited from the earliest days of settlement in southern England. Archeological evidence dates from Paleolithic times (40,000 to 10,000 years BCE). And evidence also exists of continuous occupation right through the Mesolithic period (ca 12,000-6,000 BCE) into the Neolithic, Bronze and Iron ages, when the peoples of the area first developed the land for agriculture, having imported these skills from mainland Europe when they arrived. They would have exploited the navigable waters of the Dart River to explore and settle the hinterland for farming as well. But it stands to reason that they would have also exploited the abundant marine, freshwater and anadromous (migrating from the ocean to freshwater to spawn, like salmon) resources of the area at the same time, setting the stage for the later town of Dartmouth's major claim to fame.

In more recent times, there were invasions by the Wessex peoples, who knew how to exploit the mineral resources of the area, the Celts, the Saxons, the Norse (Vikings) and the Normans, with all of these cultures blending to form the heritage of the people of the South Hams area of Devon today. These are the strains that flow through my blood and characterise my DNA.

Dartmouth as such did not exist as an established town at the time that the Domesday Book census was taken in 1086 following the Norman conquest. However, the area known as Townstal, on the height of land above Dartmouth proper did exist, and for very good reason. With all of these invading forces coming through the area, it only made sense to build your habitations away from the river, on the heights, where marauding bands could be seen long enough in advance of their arrival by water to take flight. Thus, the oldest part of Dartmouth, as we know it today, is the area surrounding St. Clement Townstal Church. This area, along with nearby Stoke Fleming, was held by Walter of Douai from Flanders (thus Stoke Fleming). Guarding, as they did, the mouth of the Dart River, these areas were of strategic importance to William the Conqueror, and their being granted to Walter is an indication of the trust placed in him by William. That said, the hilly terrain was not ideally suited for farming and held little economic value.

St. Clement Townstal Church, which was one of two churches attended by the Morey family when they moved to Dartmouth before they shifted exclusively to the more conveniently located St. Saviour's, did not exist until around 1198, except possibly as a wooden structure. Thus, it was predated by St. Gabriel's in Stoke Gabriel by about a century. Ray Freeman, in her book "Dartmouth and its Neighbours", explains the lengthy process of the coming into existence of St. Saviour's:

> *"In 1286, when Edward I visited Dartmouth, the burgesses took the chance to petition the king for permission to build a church down by the waterside in Clifton, because of the 'very*

great fatigue of their bodies' in going up to the one at Townstal."

But the church opposed the move, fearing that the mother church would fall into disuse and, lacking regular contributions from the wealthier townspeople, would eventually fall into ruins. Chapels were built and used by the gentry down by the river without authority for over one hundred years before an agreement was finally reached between the church and the town and construction of St. Saviour's began. Even then, construction was ongoing from about 1400 until completion around 1469. While there is at least one Morey burial still to be found in the churchyard of St. Clement Townstal (see below), and probably many more that have since been lost to time, it was in St. Saviour's where the majority of Morey baptisms and marriages took place and, indeed, it is in St. Saviour's Churchyard where Mary Graham, the wife of my immigrant ancestor Matthew Morry, was laid to rest beside her brother, Christopher Graham, and members of their extended families.

Another Mary Morrey was the 4th great grandmother of Ray Dickson, shown here with his late wife, Margaret, who brought us together through her research. Mary [Downing] was the wife of Capt. Richard Morrey, a first cousin of Matthew Morry, my immigrant ancestor. Thus, Ray and I are seventh cousins. Richard was also involved in the Newfoundland codfish trade but did not settle in Newfoundland. Ray continues to live in Devon. On a rainy day in October 2006, Ray and I stood shoulder to shoulder beside the graves of our respective 4th great grandmothers who both married Morey mariners involved in the Newfoundland trade; an extremely moving experience.

```
          "SACRED
       to the Memory of
          MARY MORREY
 who departed this life Feby 14 1841
          Aged 77 Years.
    ALSO THE INFANT DAUGHTER OF
     Gilbert and Caroline Baddeley
     who died 17th of Feby 1848.
              ALSO
   MARY PRINN Daughter of the Above
         Died March 13 - 1877
              AGED 87"
```
Figure 15. The Grave of Mary Morrey St. Clement Churchyard

The Early Days of English Fishing and Settlement in Newfoundland

History books and historians differ on whether John Cabot and/or his self-promoting son, Sebastian, were the first Europeans after the Vikings to make landfall in North America when they arrived in 1497. Many believe that the Cabots were actually instructed on the route that they took, if not actually piloted, by a fisherman or fishermen, possibly from the Basque country, who had already learned of the rich fishing grounds of the Grand Banks, but had kept it a secret in order to make the best commercial gain from it for themselves.

Be that as it may, the commercial draw of a massive new resource of cod within relatively easy reach of the west coast of Europe (once one learned how to make use of the prevailing winds and currents of the spring and fall in the North Atlantic) soon resulted in a massive influx of fishermen on the Banks, primarily from Spain, Portugal and France. English fish merchants were slow off the mark, comparatively speaking, and really didn't begin to prosecute this lucrative resource in a big way long before Sir Humphrey Gilbert laid claim to the whole land for Queen Elizabeth on August 5, 1583. Historians tell us he was met in what is now the Harbour of St. John's by thirty-six fishing vessels, few of which were from England, but that did not deter him from his task. The following year full-blown war, rather than what was essentially a perennial undercurrent of hostilities, broke out between Catholic Spain and Protestant England. Privateers were commissioned on both sides to harass the commercial shipping of the other nation. Ray Freeman tells us that Carew Gilbert, brother of Sir Humphrey, and Sir Bernard Drake, a distant relative of Sir Francis, led an expedition to capture all the Spanish and Portuguese vessels that they could on the Grand Banks and in coastal waters off of Newfoundland, most of which were unarmed and unprepared.

As a consequence, the playing field was left empty and to fill it the fishery was opened to any Englishman who could afford to fit out a ship, not just the chosen few from London who had held monopolies up to that time. It was during this period that the rough and tumble provincials like Arthur Holdsworth of Dartmouth moved into the void and made a place for themselves in the history books. As Freeman puts it:

"It was the Newfoundland fishing industry which provided the wealth of Dartmouth for the next 200 years."

John Morey and his kin came into the picture at the end of those two hundred years when the best pickings were already taken. It should be noted that privateering was not a one-sided venture and Thomas Newman, the *pater familias* of the Newfoundland Newman merchants, lost a new 120-ton ship to Turkish pirates in 1615 and other merchants in Dartmouth lost a further 10 vessels worth a total of £8,000 ($2.25 Million in today's money) during this period of ongoing hostilities.

The other great families of merchants, politicians and clergy, in Dartmouth in those days were the Searles and the Holdsworths. The latter, of course, were well known in Newfoundland and were intimately connected to the Newmans in business and through multiple intermarriages. The former family did not participate in the Newfoundland codfish trade in any meaningful manner but rather earned their fortune the old-fashioned way, by inheritance! John Searle and Arthur Holdsworth (the second of many by that name who figure in the history of Dartmouth) were bitter archrivals for power in Dartmouth. No doubt the old money contempt for the *nouveau riche* also had something to do with the disdain in which Searle held the entire Holdsworth dynasty. But there must have also been a tinge of jealousy because his rival, Arthur Holdsworth, and his sons and grandsons, occupied all the important positions of power in Dartmouth for over a century, including occupying the largely ceremonial office of Governors of Dartmouth Castle (five Holdsworths held this position), election to the House of Commons (Arthur Howe Holdsworth), Mayors of the town (several Holdsworths, including the very first to come to Dartmouth, were elected to this position) and Ministers of the church (Henry and Robert Holdsworth, vicars of Townstal). It was this same Arthur Holdsworth who was the fishing admiral in St. John's in 1700. Centuries later he had a street named in his honour in that city. He repopulated the outports of the southern shore, including Ferryland, on which his income depended at that time, after the destruction and abandonment of these communities at the hands of Jacques-François de Brouillon and Pierre Le Moyne d'Iberville in 1696. It was also he who built the stone house in Ferryland that three generations later became the property of Matthew Morry's grandson, John Henry Morry.

In his book, "Old Newfoundland – A History to 1843", Patrick O'Flaherty tells us that

> *"In 1697, Arthur Holdsworth sailed the NICHOLAS from Dartmouth with 100 passengers returning to Newfoundland following the disruption of their residence by the French. To those people, Newfoundland was home."*

And as quoted in W. Gordon Handcock's book "Soe Long as There Comes Noe Women", George Larkin, a contemporary of Arthur Holdsworth, says:

> *"I am credibly informed that this person, and one or two more that constantly use the Newfoundland trade, in the beginning of the year make it their business to ride from one Market Town to another in the West of England on purpose to get... passengers..."*

reporting that, in one year alone (1701), Holdsworth brought over 236 passengers, most of whom would have been bye-boat keepers[12]. Although these efforts were officially frowned upon at the time, without them Newfoundland might have wound up being French instead of English.

---

[12] A bye-boat keeper owned his own small fishing craft and employed his own crew but depended on the larger merchants to provide them transportation on their schooners, brigs and other larger sailing vessels to get from Europe to Newfoundland and back.

Figure 16. Arthur Holdsworth ca 1700

Other families that participated in the Newfoundland trade usually in partnership with either the Newmans or the Holdsworths included the Hunts, Roopes, Brookings and Teagues.

The heyday of the Newfoundland fishery for the English, primarily the "gentlemen adventurers" from the West Country, came in the 1600s. They set sail largely from ports in Devon such as Dartmouth, Poole, and Plymouth in South Devon, Barnstable in North Devon and Bristol, though in many cases they were bankrolled, at least in part, by partners in London. Lesser ports like Topsham, Paignton and Bideford also played their part in sending ships and men to the Newfoundland fishery, and inland market towns like Newton Abbot served as recruitment centres. Keep in mind that these latter ports may not have been foremost in the fishery but according to Tony Colvin and Jenny Pearson, in their monograph "Topsham to Newfoundland,

> *"In 1699, Topsham sent 34 ships with 70 boats to Newfoundland, second only to London's 71 ships".*

However, once again the so-called "London" ships would not have sailed from there but rather from one of the primary ports in the southwest. That said, these authors also report that in 1700, Benedict Stafford of Exeter, or more properly its port, Topsham, was the fishing admiral for the year in Aquaforte. They note that Topsham merchants and vessels tended to dominate in St. John's and Bay Bulls as well, whilst Dartmouth dominated in Ferryland, Renews and Fermeuse, with some competition from Teignmouth, Barnstable and Bideford.

Different West Country ports focussed their energies on different parts of the coast of Newfoundland. Most of the merchants whose vessels sailed from Dartmouth headed for the east coast of the Avalon Peninsula, the nearest landfall to their home ports. And it was thus these adventurers, more so than the well-known colonisers such as George Calvert (later Lord Baltimore), William Vaughan and John Guy, all of whose attempts were ultimately failures, whose activities, in fact, led to the population of the Southern Shore. Whether that was their original intent or not is also a hotly debated topic amongst historians.

As a descendant of one of the latter-day, though smaller scale, West Country Merchants, I must admit to some regret that this English heritage has largely been lost in the modern promotion of the "Irish Loop" around the Southern Shore, which celebrates the later settlement of the region by the Irish. English merchants employed Irish "boys" (a pejorative term in that many were grown men) to fish for them when they could no longer find sufficient numbers of English fishermen willing to make the voyage for the wages they were prepared to pay. Eventually, Irish bye-boat keepers and merchants also came to this part of Newfoundland in large numbers. W. Gordon Handcock tells us that by 1795 "Cole's statistics for the Ferryland district totalled 1536 Catholics [one can pretty well say "Irish"] and 394 Protestants [likewise, substitute "English]", so already the nature of the country had turned even before Matthew Morry set down permanent roots there.

Today, virtually everyone who comes to Newfoundland on vacation believes that it was the Irish that settled the country, especially if they spend a good deal of their time on the Southern Shore, because the accent and culture in that area are pure Irish. Or so they believe.

In fact, an ethnographer would shatter that illusion. Much of that mixed accent and pronunciation, and many of the words and phrases still in common use, are straight out of Devon. In his little book, "The Devonshire Accent", Clement Martin gives us many examples of this. Whilst much of the pronunciation heard on the southern shore, and many of the words and expressions, came over from Ireland, more than most people believe, there is also a fair measure of Devon in it too. Reading this little book, I was constantly hearing my own grandfather's voice saying the same things in the same accent four generations after the arrival of Matthew Morry in Newfoundland from Devon.

And as a last aside on this topic, one example given, viddy or vitty (meaning fitting, proper, well-made, correct, etc.), is quite possibly the derivation of the place name Quidi Vidi, something I have never seen suggested in any of the books I have read that discuss that unusual name.

Figure 17. Ken Peacock and Howard Morry, Ferryland, 1951

In addition to the spoken language that carried over from Devon to Newfoundland, my grandfather, Howard Leopold Morry, could sing by heart dozens of old folk songs that came over from Devon four generations earlier. Many of these were recorded by ethnographer and musicologist Kenneth Peacock during the 1950s and 1960s, and 14 of the 19 songs eventually made it into his three-volume manuscript, "Songs of the Newfoundland Outports".[13]

---

[13] A small number of the songs from this collection, including one sung by my father Thomas Graham Morry, ("The Sealers' Ball") appeared on an LP by the same name in 1984. Unfortunately, none sung by Dad Morry appeared on that LP as it came twelve years after his death. But a CD was eventually produced

Figure 18. Higher Street and Foss Street, Dartmouth ca 1800

in 2000 (though not available anywhere today it seems) on which 268 of the 517 originally recorded songs can be heard, including those by Dad Morry. And in 2016, Anna Kearney Guigné, who was evidently partly responsible for the production of the CD, published a book entitled "The Forgotten Songs of the Newfoundland Outports" in which she publishes more of the Ken Peacock collection that never made it into the first 3 volumes, including three of the remaining five songs contributed by Dad Morry. One of these old English folk songs, The Farmer's Boy, sung by Dad Morry in 1951, can be found by a simple search on YouTube.

Figure 19. Dartmouth from St. Clement Townstal ca 1900

Dartmouth in the Early 18th Century

By the time that John Morey and his second wife Elizabeth Matthews were raising their family in Dartmouth in the 1730s and 1740s, the Newfoundland salt cod fishery that had enriched the few and provided a livelihood to the many in the West Country was already past its zenith. Historians differ on the reasons for this decline. It is hard to imagine that a fishery this vast could have been laid low by simple fishing gear like handlines, virtually the only form of fishing gear used at the time. But it is a well-recorded fact that there were long periods in the mid-18th century when the northern cod stock failed to appear in its usual vast numbers on the fishing grounds off Newfoundland, whether due to fishing pressure or environmental factors. Other economic and socio-political forces in Europe also played a hand. As Ginny Campbell says in "Dartmouth Through Time":

> *"Much of the new wealth [in Dartmouth] came initially from the Newfoundland cod fleet, which was later extended into a triangular trade route taking cod to Spain and Portugal, and bringing port, wine and fruit back to England in the eighteenth century."*

Martin Wilcox (Fishing & Fishermen – A Guide for Family Historians) tells us that the reason the English vessels were initially slow off the mark taking advantage of the Grand Bank fishery was that they already had lucrative fisheries closer at hand on the coast of Great Britain and off Iceland. But, when the English herring and pilchard stocks became overfished and depleted toward the end of the 16th century, this provided the incentive that investors needed to fit out vessels for the distant fishery on the Grand Banks. Not that the salt cod itself formed a major replacement in the English diet. He notes that:

> *"Cured fish, in fact, has rarely been a major item of consumption in Britain, and its importance to the fisheries has been based on exports, whose markets also shaped the industry."*

Another socio-political factor to consider that has a direct bearing on the strong connections between England, Newfoundland and Portugal specifically is explained by Will and Ariel Durant in Volume VIII – *The Age of Louis XIV* – of their *magnum opus, The Story of Civilization*:

> *"Pedro II [King of Portugal] strengthened ties with England by the Methuen Treaty (1703): each nation agreed to give preferential tariffs to the other; Portugal would import manufactured goods from England [including salt cod], England would import wine and fruit from Portugal."*

The authors explain that the initial impetus behind this treaty had been the almost constant warfare during the previous century between England and Spain, on the one hand, and Portugal and Spain on the other, culminating in England's assistance to Portugal in finally winning its independence from Spain by the Treaty of Lisbon in 1688. In part, this assistance was afforded due to the fact that Charles II had married Catherine of Braganza, a member of the Portuguese royal family.

The list of products returned from the continent to England should have included more importantly salt, which was in short supply in England, and large quantities of which were needed for the production of dried cod, as opposed to the "green" lightly salted cod produced on the Grand Banks by vessels from Spain, Portugal and France.

Ginny Campbell goes on to say that the decline in the cod fishery by the beginning of the nineteenth century was partially offset by the shipbuilding industry in Dartmouth, but really the boom was over for this seaside town. Indeed, Ray Freeman notes that Between 1803 and 1810, two prominent shipbuilders, Robert Newman (see below in his court case against Matthew Morry) and Tanner went bankrupt.

Figure 20. "Prosperity to Hooks and Lines"

Presented to Arthur Holdsworth, 1723

So there seems to have been mixed prospects for anyone moving to Dartmouth from the mid-1700s onward. Perhaps that note of gloom was not apparent when John Morey seems to have made the final move there from Stoke Gabriel likely around 1729 after his first wife, Elizabeth Stone, died.

John Morey (1711-1751)

5th Great Grandfather

It is fortuitous for the Newfoundland Morry line that this John Morey decided to stick it out and raise a family in Dartmouth with his wife, Priscilla Harvey. For it was from here that his son,

Matthew Morry, struck out to make his fortune in the Newfoundland trade.

Although Dartmouth was a much larger centre of population than Stoke Gabriel, somewhat surprisingly, John and his family did not show up much more on the radar here than previous generations had done in Stoke Gabriel. To be sure, church register entries are more consistent. But there are still no records of taxation and no census returns of any kind on which they might have appeared. Nor were they apparently in business, as the name does not appear in any business directories of the day. The only clue to their presence, therefore, other than the church records, is the somewhat apocryphal mention of John's appointment as Tidesman and Boatsman. Perhaps additional research on that line of employment will one day provide greater clarity.

In the time of his son, Matthew, Dartmouth Borough Council Land Tax Assessments, which apparently only date back to 1747, give details on any recipients of public emoluments, such as would be the case for a Tidesman and Boatsman. These Assessments, which can be viewed on microfiche at the Southwest Heritage Trust in Great Moor House, Exeter, do not, however, show any indication of taxes being assessed against John Mory or anyone with a similar name from 1747 until Matthew appears on the books much later in the 1780s. Since even renters and not just property owners are included in these rolls, it would seem that the accommodations occupied by John and his family must either have been very modest or perhaps were outside the purview of the Borough Council at some distance from town.

John only lived to be forty years of age and his time was spent almost exactly divided between Stoke Gabriel and Dartmouth, evidently, if we assume that the family moved shortly before the time of his mother's death, her last child being born in Dartmouth in 1727, as discussed in the previous chapter. However, his working years would have been spent entirely in Dartmouth and the lion's share of work opportunities in the Town of Dartmouth was marine related. Also, as suggested from the discussion in regard to his father's employment, it seems most likely that it was this John and not his father who was appointed as a Tidesman and Boatsman in 1744, a position of some importance with a government emolument. W. Gordon Handcock tells us that places like Dartmouth:

> *"were places wherein dwelt families who over many generations followed the sea...In the Torbay-Dartmouth area, names such as Carter...Morry...families for whom the normal trade to which sons and grandsons followed earlier generations in their life cycles as a matter of class tradition and hereditary succession."*

It would, therefore, have been almost axiomatic that our immigrant ancestor, his son, Matthew Morry, would pursue a marine trade and, not only that but that he would not start on the bottom rung of the ladder but would be accorded some extraordinary opportunities in terms of the first work experience offered to him. This could, at least in part, explain his rapid rise in position on board the vessels on which he served in the Newfoundland codfish trade, as elaborated in the next chapter.

Priscilla, his wife, is a bit of an enigma. She may not have hailed from Dartmouth. There were no church baptism records of a Priscilla Harvey (by any conceivable spelling of the name) in Dartmouth at this time, according to online sources at least. There were many people of that surname found in marriages and burials in Dartmouth, but there were no baptismal records for any of them either. This suggests two possibilities. First, perhaps they all hailed from elsewhere; this seems unlikely, as there were far too many of them to have all showed up *en masse* at about the same time. Secondly, and this seems a more likely possibility, they were not members of the Church of England. If they were Quakers, Dissenters (Methodists) or Roman Catholics, there would be little chance of finding their baptism records; at least not in an online search. Some records of these non-conformist faiths do exist, but they have not been made public and may be very difficult to obtain. It should be noted that John's sister, Mary, married a man named John Harvey, quite possibly Priscilla's brother, and there is no baptismal record for him either.

Whatever the reason for the missing baptismal records, marriage and burial records for Priscilla do appear in the register of St. Clement. On the other hand, baptismal records for each of their children are found in the St. Saviour's register. And all but their last son, Matthew, who is buried in Forge Hill Cemetery in Ferryland, along with his grandson John, are buried at St. Clement's. The reason for this apparent separation in the church of attendance and place of burial is not known. It must be presumed that the small churchyard at St. Saviour's was no longer open to new burials, whilst the cemetery in Townstal had ample room for expansion and is, in fact, still in use today. It is not surprising that the family would choose to attend services at St. Saviour's as it was in the heart of the town, rather than on the height of land coming into the town in Townstal, a difficult climb for anyone to make every Sunday.

John and Priscilla had a very hard time with the births of their children. Four of their first five children died in early childhood, most shortly after being born. John survived to manhood but died at twenty-nine, unmarried and childless. Matthew's only surviving sibling, his older sister Elizabeth, lived a long life, along with her husband, Samuel Hoyles, but they died childless as well. So, but for Matthew, this line would have died out in Devon and the Morrys of Newfoundland who later spread throughout North America and beyond would never have existed.

CHAPTER SIX - STRIKING OUT FOR PARTS UNKNOWN

Matthew Morry I (1750-1836)

4th Great Grandfather

Now we come to the man who was the inspiration and motivation for writing this book. I mentioned earlier that a principal objective of writing the book was to fill a void in the many fine compendiums of Newfoundland history concerning the role of the minor West Country Merchants who played a significant part in the development and settlement of outport Newfoundland between when the absentee major English merchant firms lost interest in Newfoundland toward the end of 18th century and the advent of Responsible Government in the Colony in 1855.

This is not to suggest that he was in any way spectacularly different from the other men like him, who filled similar roles in every outport around the coast. Quite the contrary. In their anthology of *"1500 individuals who have influenced the development of Newfoundland and Labrador as a colony, country and province…"* the editors of the "Dictionary of Newfoundland and Labrador Biography" did not see fit to mention Matthew Morry, nor any Morry for that matter, nor even Caplin Bay as a place of significance to early settlement[14]. I suspect that, in many respects, all of these small-scale West Country Merchants bore considerable similarities to one another. They were all self-made men, most likely with limited formal education but a solid education before the mast, tough with those who depended on them to supply the necessities of life, but equally stinting in extending the comforts of life to themselves and their families.

In Matthew's case, and possibly in the case of many of the others, there were also at least a couple of negative personality traits that had a great bearing on how they conducted themselves. I must emphasise that I am basing the following on an intensive study of his nature, deduced primarily from lengthy tracts submitted in Court which were either his own words or those of lawyers representing his sentiments and opinions, as well as similar tracts presented by those in opposition to him in these court cases. It may be argued that this is a narrow base of information on which to form an analysis of the personality of a person now deceased more than 175 years ago. But since it is all that we have to fall back on in order to develop a clearer picture of the man, it is my feeling that these impressions are at least as valid as many statements made by historians on the nature of other historical figures.

I believe that he was a person, in the immortal words of Robert Browning, "whose reach exceeded his grasp" all too often,

---

[14] They did however mention the pirate, Peter Easton, in reference to Ferryland, though most historians now believe that the stories of his visiting that part of the island are probably apocryphal.

resulting ultimately, at least partially, in the failure of his company. He also seems to have been naïve to affairs of business and too willing to trust others of greater intellect, or at least greater education and station in life, which also combined to end the 35-year reign of his business partnership and resulted in him finding himself in Court repeatedly and interminably in England and Newfoundland. And, unfortunately, and here I believe this may indeed have been a common trait of men like him, there seems to have been a hardness in his morality when it came to his dealings with the financial well-being of others over whom he had an ethical duty and a trust to protect. But all of this will emerge and be discussed at greater length below. For now, let's turn to what we know about Matthew and his family from the church records in Dartmouth.

First of all, as stated above, Matthew was the only member of his family to have children. The importance of this cannot be overstated, from my somewhat biased standpoint, since I and at least two thousand other people would never have existed were it not for this. That is the approximate number of his direct descendants presently in my family tree file. Nor would there have been any Devon Morrys in Newfoundland. Some of his cousins and uncles did travel there, but none settled and raised families. And the diaspora of Morrys that eventually took place to the rest of mainland North America and beyond would never have occurred.

That said, he and his first wife, the mother of all of his children, Mary Graham, who was the daughter of another seafaring family in Dartmouth, had a relatively small family for the day, only six (or possibly seven; more on this possibility later) children, and of those, only three, in turn, had families. His marriage to his second wife, Anne Carter, a Newfoundland-born daughter of the first West Country merchant who came and stayed on the southern shore, came late in life for both of them, when no further children were possible. Which makes the total number of his descendants in five generations all the more remarkable.

Their family group sheets as they presently stand are found in Appendix 2. Note that Anne Carter was twice married prior to Matthew and children by her previous marriages do not appear on their family group sheet.

Mary Graham and Her Kin

As stated above, the family of his first wife, Mary Graham, was heavily involved in the marine trades, specifically but not solely as seamen and Masters on vessels plying the Newfoundland codfish trade. Her father and brother, both named Christopher, and another brother named Francis were in turn Masters on vessels sometimes involved with Newfoundland and sometimes coasting around Britain, with occasional forays to the continent. In fact, Christopher the younger and Francis were, from time to time, the Master on vessels owned by Matthew Morry. Another brother, John, also served as Mate on a vessel owned by Matthew Morry. Through their diligence and hard work, the family became reasonably well-to-do for their day and respected members of the Dartmouth community.

The Graham family was not one of long-term residence in Dartmouth. It is not known where Christopher the father was born, but it was not in Dartmouth, and probably not in southern England. He may have been from the border counties where there were notable ports for young men to learn the ropes, metaphorically and literally. There are church registers in that part of the country with baptism records for boys named Christopher Graham at more or less the time that he should have been born, but there is no way to connect him with any of those records.

But ultimately, family lore had it that this family came from Scotland, as the name suggests, and that they were a part of the clan associated with "Bluidy Clavers", the pejorative name applied by his enemies to John Graham, 1st Viscount Dundee, the 7th Laird of Claverhouse. These more than likely apocryphal tales were disseminated by the maiden aunts of my grandfather and if there is one thing less reliable than an old wives' tale it has to be an old spinster's tale! In any event, there is not a shred of credible evidence to make the connection.

Which is not to say that these tales are untrue. Once again it must always be remembered when examining oral history that a lack of evidence must never be used to prove or disprove such stories. But the sad reality is that there is a remarkable void of family papers that have come down to us in the Morry family, considering that the family had long been a part of the merchant class. And there is a well-documented reason for that but I will have to depart briefly from the chronology and geography of our story to provide the reader with the answer.

The Lost Accounts and Papers of Matthew Morry & Co.

The management of Matthew Morry & Co. was handed down through the two subsequent Matthews, son and grandson, in Caplin Bay. When the last of these died, his home, known as Athlone, became the residence of a maiden daughter known as Miss Lizzie Morry. During her youth, the family had taken in a poor boy from a family unable to support all their children, a common practice in outport Newfoundland right up to the immediate past generation, and possibly still occurring in a few cases today. His name was Alfred Canning and he became like a brother to Elizabeth. When she was getting on in years, Alfred's son, Leonard, and his wife came to live with her and take care of her. A few months before she passed away in 1930, she signed a "death-bed Will", which was never contested, and which left the house and all of its contents, the lands and the waterside premises to Leonard and his wife. Elizabeth's only surviving relative was her brother Henry, and he was by then living in British Columbia and could not easily intercede in this matter, even if he had wished to do so. My grandfather made an attempt to recover the Morry family papers from the house, but was not successful, except for managing to take a small number of personal letters belonging to Elizabeth. The papers were of no value to the Cannings or anyone else, and no doubt they were used to light the fire or were otherwise destroyed. Thus, there are no records of the Morry enterprise in existence today. Some of these papers may have told the tale concerning the origins of Mary's family. If so, we will never know now.

As an aside related to this loss of the Morry papers, in the summer of 2018 I stumbled upon the answer to a riddle that had perplexed the family for generations. While conducting some research at the Centre for Newfoundland Studies and the associated Archives and Special Collections unit at the Queen Elizabeth II Library of Memorial University I discovered that there was a relatively new series of folders referred to as "Name Files" in which odd notes, mostly copies of newspaper clippings, on families of note in Newfoundland are added from time to time. One of them was labelled simply "Morry Family". In it I found a note on file written by Nimshi Crewe, the former provincial archivist mentioned previously. This note indicated that he had "recently" (sometime in the mid-1960s) purchased a set of the complete works of William Shakespeare published in 1790 from an unnamed source in Calvert and that, in at least four of the volumes, appeared the signatures of "Matthew Morry Jr. the 3rd" and "Mrs.

Ann Morry Snr.". This was what family history researchers refer to as a "Eureka! moment." I and others in the family had been told of the existence of these books by Dad Morry and indeed he had endeavoured to secure the return of them from the house in Calvert after Miss Lizzie's death but had not been successful. No one knew what had become of them until I accidentally stumbled upon this note some eighty years later. Obviously, they had been sold by the Canning family to Nimshi, who in turn donated or sold them to Memorial University.

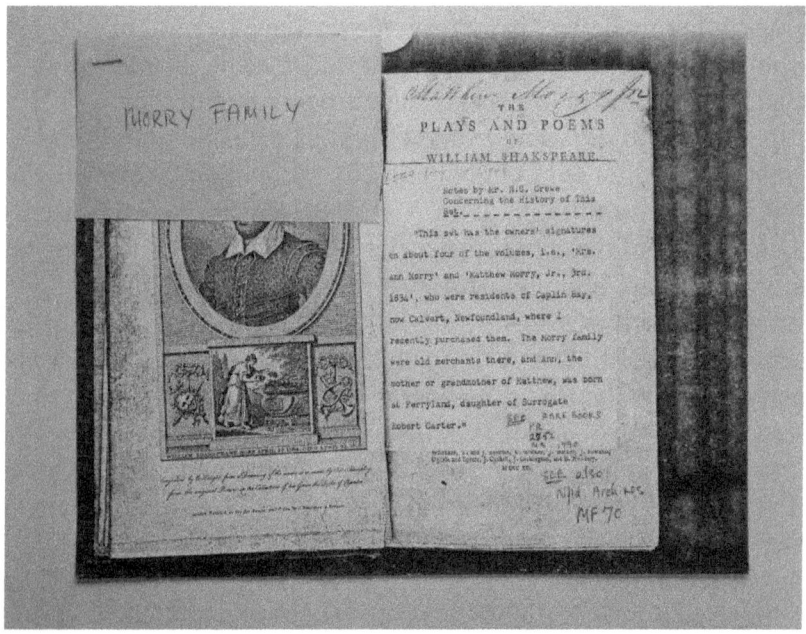

Figure 21. N. Crewe Note in Volume of William Shakespeare

I was privileged to be allowed to view and to take photographs of the entire set of these books, which were eleven in number, and which, as it turns out, contained the signatures of Matthew Morry, the immigrant, his second wife, Ann [Carter] Morry, who signed as "Mrs. Ann Morry Senr.", his son Matthew, who signed his name as "Matthew Morry Jr.", and his grandson, who signed his name as "Matthew Morry Jr., 3rd." What a remarkable family heirloom, and what a relief to know that it was not lost forever as we had thought.

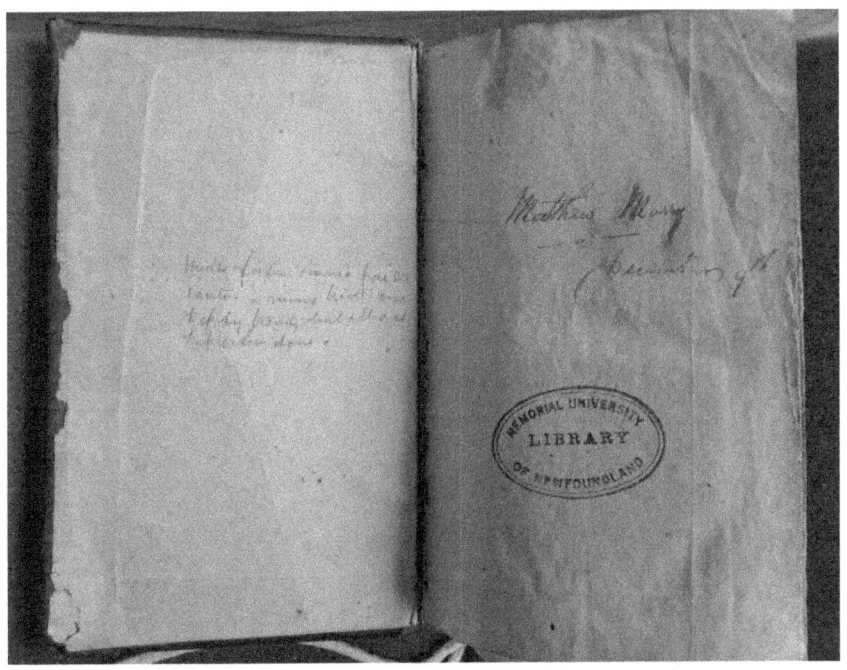

Figure 22. Vol. 3 with Signature of Matthew Morry I

Figure 23. Vol. 4 with Signature of Matthew Morry Jr.

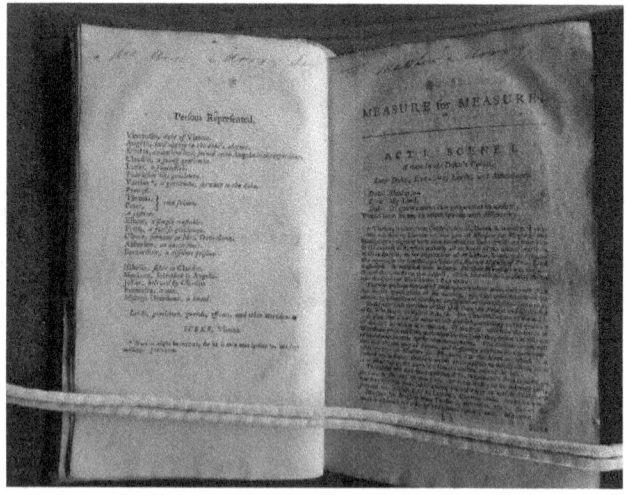

Figure 24. Vol. 2 of Complete Works of Shakespeare

Dedication by Mrs. Ann Morry Senr. to Matthew Morry Jr. 3rd.

Returning to our storyline in Dartmouth, Mary was only forty-six when she died and it was originally thought she had died in childbirth, but eventually, it was determined that her last child had been born more than a year prior, so there is no explanation for her seemingly early death. She is buried in the churchyard of St. Saviour's, along with their daughter, Priscilla. Beside her grave is that of her brother, Christopher, and several of his descendants. Her gravestone was seriously damaged by an errant German bomb that fell nearby during WWII but fortunately, one of Dad Morry's aunts, Jane Josephine [Morry} Gray, had visited Dartmouth before the war and taken down the inscriptions on several gravestones and monuments pertinent to the family, including this one. Here is how it reads:

"Sacred to the memory of Mary Morry the wife of Matthew Morry, Merchant of this town who was the sincere Christian, the faithful wife, the affectionate mother, and the true friend universally loved and sincerely lamented, who departed this life on 29 October 1796. Aged 46 Years. Also sacred to the memory of Priscilla, daughter of the above-named Matthew and Mary Morry, and wife of Wm. Sweetland of Ferryland in the island of Newfoundland, now of Dartmouth, Merchant, who no less virtuous and esteemed departed this life on the 19 day of December 1820. Aged 37 years."

Figure 25. Mary [Graham] Morry's Gravestone, St. Saviour's

A Possible Birth in Newfoundland

As will be described in greater detail shortly, Matthew Morry became the Master and Commander of vessels plying the Newfoundland codfish trade in his early twenties, quite a remarkable circumstance. In fact, his first commission would have been more or less at the same time that he and Mary married on March 1st, 1773. No doubt there was a direct connection, as this would have afforded him a healthy and stable income. In those days, it was not uncommon for the Master of a vessel to take his wife and even some of their children on long voyages to maintain closer ties. But it is not known if Mary accompanied Matthew to Newfoundland on any of his voyages. There is only one clue to this possibility.

Aunt Jean's family group sheet for this family showed a child I could not place in the Dartmouth church registers, Honor Caroline, said to have been baptized on October 4, 1791. There was a child of that name in the register of Flavel Congregational Independent Meeting House in Dartmouth, but Matthew's family was Anglican and their children were all baptised at St. Saviour's. The registers at Dissenter churches were notoriously haphazard and this was no exception. It said "Oct 4 1791 Honor Caroline daughter of Mr. Morry". Not particularly helpful. Through diligent research on the part of Margaret Dickson (mentioned above), I was eventually able to dismiss this record as the child in question was assuredly a relative, but not a daughter of Matthew and Mary, instead being a daughter of his cousin Richard Morrey, another sea captain, and Richard's wife, Mary Downing, who was a Dissenter.

However, I found it hard to accept that Aunt Jean, a seasoned family historian, could have made such an elementary error, so I kept searching for another Honor Morry. It was at this time that I was scrutinising the early records of the Anglican Cathedral in St. John's to see if I could find any records of family there. Lo and behold, I came upon a record that I convinced myself was proof of the existence of a child named Honor in Matthew and Mary's family, and incidentally, proof that Mary had come to Newfoundland at least once. That record read: "Hon^r. Dr. Mark Moary & Mary Dec. 29" in the oldest version of the register in existence and "Hon$^{'r}$. D^r of Mark Morey of Mary [Dec.] 29" in a later transcript, both dated in the year 1778. I could not accept that the man's name was Mark because, after years of research with the international "One Name" Morey research group headed by Geoffrey Williams (mentioned above) we had never once encountered a Mark of that surname (by any spelling) in over one hundred thousand records. I suspected that it was being misread and was actually "Matt", not "Mark". But after years of attempts, when I was finally permitted to see the original register in my own two hands in the archives of the Anglican Cathedral, my hopes were dashed, because I realised that the transcribers and the poor-quality microfilms and photocopies I had previously seen did not lie and the man whose name appeared in the register was indeed "Mark".

Being obstinate, I still do not believe it! I believe that the Minister or his assistant who entered this baptism into the register made a mistake in writing the man's name and that it should have been "Matt" for Matthew. Of course, that same mistake would have been copied over in the second transcript, so having two versions of the baptism record does not lend any more credibility to the details. One reason for being so obstinate is that, at this very period in the development of Matthew Morry's career as a mariner, there is suddenly, for no apparent reason, an absence of records of him for over a year on board any vessels travelling between Devon and Newfoundland. Similarly, there is a long gap between the birth of their first son, John, in 1776 and the child next baptised at St. Saviour's, Priscilla in 1783. Of course, there could be other explanations for these gaps in the records, but I hold onto the faint hope that this was because he spent a year in Newfoundland at that time with his wife Mary whilst she was giving birth to their second child, Honor. If so, she would have been the first Morry born in the New World.

But let's set aside the question of the existence of a child named Honor for now and have a look at the other members of this family.

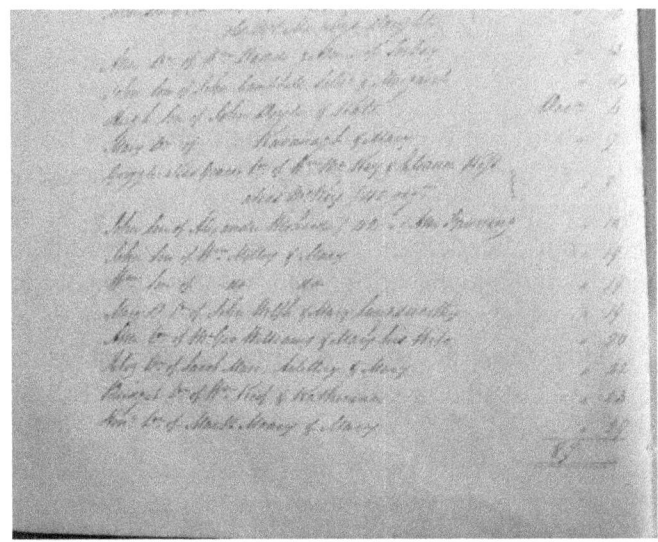

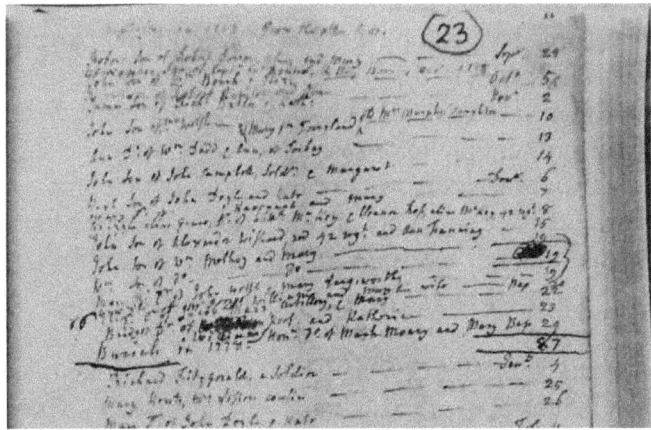

Figure 26. Two Baptism Records for Honor Moary

John Morry - Privateer

The first-born son was an interesting character – for his short life! John was the only one of the children of Matthew and Mary who was baptised at St. Petrox rather than St. Saviour's. St. Petrox was the church attended by the gentry in Dartmouth (e.g. the Holdsworths) and, having just earned his Master papers, it would seem that Matthew could foresee himself becoming one of them. But apparently, those delusions of grandeur did not last for long because all of his other children were baptised at St. Saviour's where they "belonged"!

John became a privateer with Letters of Marque from the Crown at least as early as the War with France at the turn of the 19th century. The record that was found to prove this was: *Register of Letters of Marque against France 1793-1815*, in which we learn that John Morry received his Letters of Marque on November 12, 1805, for the Schooner ALEXANDER, 100 tonnes, with a crew of 25 and ordinance of ten - 12-pound cannon on board. Whether he had such a commission before that date, or whether he served in a lower role than Master on other vessels prior to that time we do not know. Toward the end of his all too brief life and career, he had been making enough money from his share of the prize money, serving as a Master and Commander, to provide himself and his small family with a very comfortable income.

Two years later, in February 1807, John was dead, under what I would characterise as suspicious circumstances. There is no burial record for him. Nor is there a burial record for his brother, Thomas Graham Morry, who died at the same time. My guess is that they got the worst of a battle with a vessel that they were attempting to seize. In any event, before his untimely demise, John had salted away a fair bit of money in Consolidated £3 Per Cent. Annuities and other investments and had a number of "Prizes" (at least half a dozen) awaiting disposal at auction according to advertisements that appeared in Trewman's Exeter Flying Post, the Ipswich Journal and the Plymouth and Cornish Advertiser the year of his death and the year prior to and following his death.

Figure 27. Auctioning One of John Morry's Prizes

As Master, his share of the prize money would have been the third largest, after the government and owners took their cuts[15]. Suffice it to say, despite his sad early demise, he left his widow and only son, John Foale Morry, well provided for. But this situation was not to last for a couple of reasons. Firstly, his wife, Mary Foale [Luke] Morry died only five months later at the age of thirty-seven. I would also characterise that death as unusual since she was young, did not die in childbirth, and was not exactly starving to death. One wonders if she may have become despondent after John's death and her early death was in some way related to that.

In any event, this left their only son, then seven years of age, an orphan. And that is the second reason for the circumstance in which John Senior left his family not being ideal comes in. Matthew Morry took charge at this point and was declared the guardian of his grandson, meaning he also took charge of his grandson's inheritance, which somehow disappeared over the coming decade before John Junior had a chance to claim it at his age of majority. The circumstances surrounding the disappearance of the inheritance money and the court cases that ensued will be fully explored below. I will also talk a little more about the involvement of John Foale Morry in the Newfoundland Trade when he became old enough to be his own man. For now, it is sufficient to say, in order to raise some suspense, that Matthew Morry and his grandson are buried together in Forge Hill Cemetery in Ferryland.

---

[15] This was another matter that found Matthew Morry in Court in 1813. The auctioneer, Joshua Rowe of Torpoint, Cornwall, apparently never did pay into the estate the monies owing from the prizes mentioned. It is possible he settled the matter out of Court with Matthew Morry, as the guardian of John Foale Luke, but if so, other Court documents do not show that Matthew ever passed the money over to the estate. More on this later.

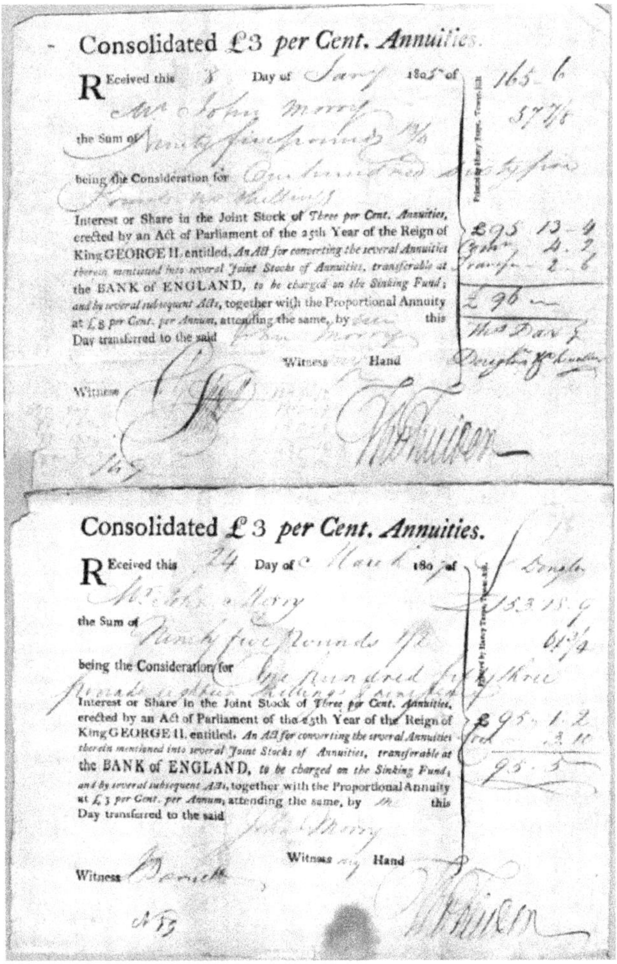

Consolidated £3 per Cent. Annuities.

REceived this 8 Day of Jan 1805 of Mr John Morry the Sum of Ninety five pounds

being the Consideration for One hundred sixty five Pounds six Shillings

Interest or Share in the Joint Stock of Three per Cent. Annuities, erected by an Act of Parliament of the 25th Year of the Reign of King GEORGE II. entitled, An Act for converting the several Annuities therein mentioned into several Joint Stocks of Annuities, transferable at the BANK of ENGLAND, to be charged on the Sinking Fund; and by several subsequent Acts, together with the Proportional Annuity at £3 per Cent. per Annum, attending the same, by me this Day transferred to the said John Morry

Witness my Hand

Witness

165 6
57 7/8
£95 13 4
4 2
2 6
£96

Consolidated £3 per Cent. Annuities.

REceived this 24 Day of March 180 of Mr John Morry the Sum of Ninety five Pounds

being the Consideration for One hundred fifty three

Interest or Share in the Joint Stock of Three per Cent. Annuities, erected by an Act of Parliament of the 25th Year of the Reign of King GEORGE II. entitled, An Act for converting the several Annuities therein mentioned into several Joint Stocks of Annuities, transferable at the BANK of ENGLAND, to be charged on the Sinking Fund; and by several subsequent Acts, together with the Proportional Annuity at £3 per Cent. per Annum, attending the same, by me this Day transferred to the said John Morry

Witness my Hand

Witness

153 18 9
61 3/4
£95 1 2
3 10
95 5

Figure 28. Two of John Morry's £3 Per Cent Annuities

Priscilla Morry and William Sweetland

Matthew and Mary's second child, if we dispense for a moment with the theoretical Honor, was Priscilla. As mentioned before, Priscilla is buried with her mother in St. Saviour's Churchyard in Dartmouth. But not because she failed to marry. In fact, she did marry and raised a family of six. However, there is good reason to believe that it was not entirely a happy marriage. Her husband was William Sweetland, who was born in Ferryland, the son of Capt. Henry J. Sweetland of Uffculme and Anne Carter, who later, after Henry's death, was to take Matthew Morry Senior as her third husband.

These three families, the Carters, Morrys and Sweetlands, were to become inseparably bound by multiple marital and business relationships. The Sweetlands were more than likely positioned in Newfoundland before Matthew Morry obtained his first grant for a fishing room in Caplin Bay, though initially at least the Sweetlands appear to have been based in Ferryland (three sons in this family, including William, Henry and Benjamin, were later to hold property in Caplin Bay and indeed were for some time partners with Matthew Morry Jr.). We know that the earliest of the Sweetlands to arrive in the area, Capt. Henry J. Sweetland, married Anne Carter around 1785. He was also one of two JPs (the other being Robert Carter) who, along with the Naval Surrogate, Capt. Edward Pellew, adjudicated at the trial which followed the Ferryland Riots in 1788[16]. Of this affair, Kevin Major, in his book

---

[16] Considered by most historians to be an internecine battle between Irish Catholic factions who favoured different priests to minister to them. They posed little, if any, threat to the English Protestant elite, but 111 men were convicted of rioting, which must have been nearly the entire Irish population of the area at the time. Four of the rioters were "transported" (more than likely

"As Near to Heaven By Sea – A History of Newfoundland and Labrador" notes:

> *"One has to question whether the Protestant elite that made up the judiciary weren't trying to contain what they saw as a Catholic threat to their authority, to rein in the Irish on the pretext that drunken males smashing in each other's skulls on the Ferryland Downs was a danger to the few [English Protestant] families and property owners."*

The Carters had been in Ferryland from at least 1742 and were in every respect the senior merchants along that part of the Southern Shore, after the Holdsworths pulled up stakes, and before Matthew arrived. Not that Matthew posed much of a challenge to their position in the community. In fact, his marriage to Anne Carter looks suspiciously like a "marriage of convenience", on his part if not on hers, to forge closer ties with the social and business leaders in the community. As for Anne, well she seems to have been in the practice of marrying sea captains, having already buried Capt. Sam Hill and Capt. Henry Sweetland and presumably having done very well financially and in terms of property holdings by these marriages. Her father also contributed to her wealth in both areas.

As stated, William Sweetland was born in Ferryland and spent most of his time there after his marriage to Priscilla, but it is debatable if she ever went there herself. Certainly, all of their children were baptised in Dartmouth at St. Saviour's. They all lived interesting and colourful, but brief lives, some being lost at

---

returned to Ireland where they had signed on), several received the customary punishment for misdemeanors of this sort of 39 lashes, and one had his house confiscated and sold to pay his £20 fine. All the rest lost their wages for the year.

sea or in foreign lands such as India. But before they reached the age of majority, their mother passed away, possibly due to birthing their last child, Mary. It is said that William effectively abandoned his Dartmouth family at that point, leaving them in the care of Morry relatives. He was later appointed a magistrate in Bonavista and remarried there. He kept a diary during part of his time as a magistrate and in it, he recorded a number of events of personal significance, including the travels and eventually the deaths of several of his children, so he did not completely forget his first family.

Before leaving this brief discussion of the family of Priscilla Ann Morry and her husband William Sweetland, I must tell an almost incredible anecdote pertaining to them. In April 2016, I attended a Devon-Newfoundland symposium in England which focussed on the connection between the two areas as a result of the fish trade. In some spare time while on a tour of Dartmouth, I stopped into the St. Saviour's churchyard to pay my respects at the graves of my fourth great grandmother, Mary [Graham] Morry and others. I noticed two women nearby seemingly struggling to find a grave and asked if I could assist them, though indeed I was far from an expert in regard to the location of graves in that cemetery. I was dumbfounded to learn that they were searching for the very gravestone that I was then standing beside. It turned out that one of them, Jennie Crisp, through an odd sequence of events, had come into possession of a family bible given by Matthew Morry to his daughter Priscilla Ann and her husband William Sweetland at the time of their marriage! Remarkably, Jennie was not even related to these people.

Figure 29. Matthew Morry's Bible

Given to daughter Priscilla, 1815

The next day, Jennie brought this bible to show me at the conference centre in Exeter. I was able to hold it in my hands and make photographs of the pages on which the family's births, marriages and deaths were recorded for three generations. This bizarre coincidence of events is a once in a lifetime occurrence for a family historian – if he is very lucky!

Thomas Graham Morry – Privateer?

Matthew and Mary's son, Thomas Graham, we have already discussed. We know little about him other than that he died at the same time as his brother John, and almost certainly suffered the same fate. His estate expenses come up in the court cases in which Matthew is embroiled with his ex-business partner, Walter Prideaux, discussed below.

Mary Morry and Arthur Kemp

Daughter Mary also married a seagoing man, Arthur Kemp, a merchant and master mariner. They had only one child, John Morry Kemp, who turned his back on the sea and became a draper, of all things[17]! I said earlier that all of Matthew and Mary's

---

[17] In his little book, "Dartmouth Industry and Banking", Ivor H. Smart notes that "The trades of drapers and mercers were less speculative than those who were caught up in the cyclical textile trade." and hence men from these trades were amongst the first owners of "Country Banks". Whether John Morry Kemp speculated in this manner is unknown.

children were baptised at St. Saviour's. This was not entirely true. Mary, for reasons unknown, was baptised at the Dissenter's Meeting House, most likely because her mother's family attended there and Matthew was away when the baptism took place. She outlived her husband and was found as an annuitant at Ford Cottage in the New Road, a very desirable part of Dartmouth, in the 1851 Census, meaning she was well provided for at his death.

Esther Graham Morry - Spinster

I will skip over Matthew Morry II for the moment and discuss his younger sister, Esther Graham Morry, the first of many to be thus named. Esther never left Dartmouth and, near as can be told from census records and the like, never worked a day in her life, even though she remained a spinster. Apparently, she was also an annuitant, but the source of her funds must have been her father since she was never married. In the 1851 and 1861 Censuses, she was occupying premises in the Crowther's Hill area of Dartmouth, another posh area occupied by people like the Newmans and Holdsworths.

Matthew Morry II – An Introduction

Finally, we have Matthew Morry J$^{r.}$ or Matthew Morry II, as we who have studied the Morry family history have come to call him, because that name, like Thomas Graham Morry and Esther Graham Morry, has recurred in every generation at least once. This was my 3rd great grandfather. Young Matthew was the only member of the family to move lock, stock and barrel with his father to Newfoundland after his mother died. Others must have come and gone, one would assume, since several of them were only infants when she died, and it would have been difficult for Matthew to have their care provided for when he was not present for much of the year. But the young Matthew was there to stay, and to become the businessman in the family. He partnered with the Sweetlands in the owning of several vessels used in their respective and common business enterprises. This Matthew Morry will be the focus of much of the last chapter of this book.

There are many fascinating stories to be told about this family and the Grahams but for now, I must restrict myself to the topic at hand, the life and times of Matthew Morry, the *pater familias* of the Morrys of North America.

Matthew Morry I's Rise as a Merchant Mariner (1771-1774)

So, let us turn our attention again to the man himself, Matthew Morry I. How did he manage to rise from humble beginnings to become a vessel owner and fish merchant of some considerable means operating out of Dartmouth and Caplin Bay/Ferryland?

To follow his career and rise from ordinary seaman to Master and Commander has been made easy thanks, once again, to the monumental work undertaken by Dr. Keith Matthews in the preparation of his "Name Files" as part of the background for his Ph.D. thesis. He carried out this research the old-fashioned way, by travelling to England and Ireland and poring over countless volumes of old records, searching for any reference to Newfoundland and the people who played a part in its development and settlement. The task was completed by doing the same for all existing records in Newfoundland as well. This body of work, which initially formed the basis of his Ph.D. research, and later became an area of research for the rest of his career, also now forms one of the major starting points for anyone conducting family history research at the Maritime History Archive (MHA) at MUN, of which he was a founding member.

The Keith Matthews "Name Files", as they are known, are an eclectic and sometimes obtuse collection of ephemera that Dr. Matthew's gathered manually, and that were later separated into individual family names by members of his family, students and other volunteers. In the case of the Morry name (by its various spellings), the collection amounts to some sixty-five pages, on each of which is recorded in his idiosyncratic shorthand a dozen or so entries of incidents he found of that name in one of many sources he studied in various British, Irish or Newfoundland archives and libraries.

The Morry Name File (M351), like all of the other Name Files, includes entries for any and all people of that particular name, by any one of its variant spellings. In most instances, and this is true for the Morry Name File, not all of the people whose histories are hinted at by the entries were related to one another. My research has shown that, in Newfoundland, there are at least three different groups of Morrys or Moreys; the line begun by Matthew Morry on the Southern Shore, being English Anglicans; the line of Moreys in the Flatrock/Torbay area, being Irish Roman Catholics; and the line of Moreys on the northeast coast, being English Methodists, or other related Protestant faiths. They migrated to these areas independently and at different times in Newfoundland's history. Nor was the Matthew Morry line always distinguishable by its unique spelling of the surname. As discussed previously, in England the spelling varied from Mory, to Morey, to Morrey, to Maury, to Morry, and probably other spellings over time and geography and even sometimes in the same family in the same generation. Indeed, members of my own grandfather's family were frequently recorded officially in church and legal documents as "Morey" as recently as the early 1900s.

So, it is important, when making use of this extremely valuable resource, to not be too hide-bound in limiting one's search to a particular spelling of a name, while at the same time not making the mistake of assuming that everyone of that surname must be related to one another.

Another element of the learning process in using these Name Files is that one must effectively learn a new language – the hieroglyphics of Keith Matthews. There is an entire volume dedicated to this at the MHA. This so-called "Abbreviation Guide" [18] amounts to over a hundred pages, similar to a dictionary, in which his short forms are listed alphabetically and explained. It takes some getting used to, but once you get the hang of it, you seldom have to turn to the guide again for an explanation.

Setting aside the other forenames in the Morry Name File, events related to Matthew Morry fill fifteen pages. Some of these pages would relate to Matthew Morry II (the son of our man), of course, but even allowing for that, there are over a hundred "hints" contained in these pages that point towards sources of information directly relevant to the marine career of Matthew Morry I. I checked each one of these in sources like the Dartmouth Muster Rolls, the Lloyd's Register of Shipping, the Exeter and Dartmouth Port Books and of course the relevant church registers in Dartmouth and Newfoundland, amongst other sources where the name appeared and was found by Keith Matthews.

Here is just one example of an entry pertaining to a critical point in the maritime career of Matthew Morry:

---

[18] *Keith Matthews Name Files, Abbreviation Guide*; unpublished manuscript; Maritime History Archive, Memorial University of Newfoundland

> *"MORRY*
> *1775 bt 98/6 Mat age 26 dtmth CAPT MARY ship ex same fm caminha 30 mar dtmth 8 sep-10 oct – 2 nov nfld 1776 7 feb dtmth fm Lisbon"*

This Board of Trade Muster Roll for 1775 and 1776 shows Matthew as Captain of the *MARY* sailing from Caminha (Portugal) to Dartmouth early in the year with whatever cargo he purchased there with the proceeds of the sale of his salt fish from Newfoundland and then turning around and sailing back to Newfoundland to begin the process again. Finally, it shows another sailing to Dartmouth from Lisbon on February 7th, 1776. This shows that he left Newfoundland and most likely sailed directly to Lisbon to trade his cargo before then returning home to Dartmouth. Though it does not say so, I believe that it may have been at this time that Matthew became the owner of the MARY, as we see him as such in one of the next records covering this period. This is a pivotal moment in his career and it is unfortunate that the record is ambiguous at this crucial time.

The entire results of the detailed analysis of Matthew Morry's maritime career based on such readings from the Keith Matthews Name File has been prepared but is too lengthy to be presented here and will ultimately be presented for publication in an appropriate journal.

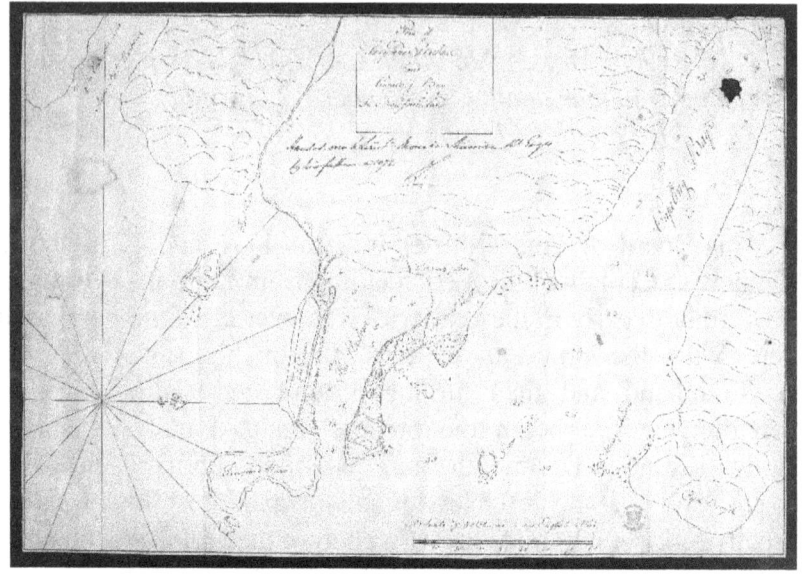

Figure 30. Plan of Ferryland and Capling [sic] Bay 1775[19]

This view is much as Matthew Morry would have known the area at the time.

To summarise the results of this analysis, it can be said with some certainty that Matthew Morry Senior's career as a Seaman,

---

[19] Reference: Titled '33,231. A-PP. Maps and plans, chiefly of fortification or surveys for military purposes. They appear (together with Nos. 33,232, 33,233) to have been collected by Lieutenant-General William Skinner, R.E. [ob. 1780], from whom they descended to Lieut. Monier Skinner, R.E., in 1872 (See add. MS. 22,875 for other copies of many of the plans in this collection.) They are: - II.14. Ferryland Harbour, and Capeling Bay, Newfoundland' in The British Library catalogue of additions to the manuscripts in the British Museum, in the years MDCCCLXXXII-MDCCCLXXXVII, Call Number: From the British Library, Add MS 33231.II.14

Mate, Captain and Ship Owner came to an end in 1821. We also know with certainty that his career began at least in 1771, 50 years prior, when he was an Able-Bodied Seaman of 21, but almost certainly began 5 to 7 years before that, the records unfortunately not being available to cover that period – a long and illustrious career. By 1773 he was Master of the MARY and by 1774 he owned her! And things developed rapidly from there.

Keith Matthew's Name File for the Morrys provides similar references to several other Morry's maritime careers, including Matthew Junior, John (Matthew Senior's son), William, his brother (believed) and George, his second cousin. But this is fodder for another line of research.

Matthew Morry & Co. (1775-1813)

Beginning in 1775, many of the entries in Lloyd's Registry and Board of Trade documents referring to Matthew Morry's career begin to speak of Matthew Morry and Company, of Dartmouth and Caplin Bay. It was through the endless court documents pertaining to the sad and rancorous demise of this company, starting in 1813 and going on for years afterwards (covered in detail in the next chapter), that we first learn of Matthew's partnership with Walter Prideaux. Before discussing what we now know to be true about this fascinating gentleman, let us recall what family lore told us about him.

In many of Dad Morry's memoirs and letters, and in the stories he told us as children, as well as in the writings that survive of several of his elders, mainly his maiden aunts, we in the family grew up knowing for a fact that our immigrant ancestor was ruined financially because of the skullduggery of a man named Walter Prideaux. In the story we all knew by heart, Matthew was a partner in a banking firm working out of the Channel Islands known as

Morry, Prideaux and Le Messurier. And we were told that this enterprise came to its end because one of the partners, Walter Prideaux, absconded with the holdings of the bank, leaving the other two partners to settle up with the depositors.

Dad Morry believed this story to be the gospel truth, and I believe Aunt Jean accepted his word for it without examination because she was not interested in such side issues to the family history, only in the ancestry itself, which was important for her duties as a Mormon.

So, it was that it fell to me as the first Morry family historian with a scientific education, in which one is trained to examine facts objectively, to examine the derivation of this story. Through lengthy research, it eventually became clear that there never was a bank by the name of Morry, Prideaux and Le Messurier in the Channel Islands.

And whilst Walter Prideaux and Peter Paint Le Messurier were both historical figures associated with the Morrys, they more than likely never knew one another. Peter Paint Le Messurier, who was indeed from the Channel Islands (St. Peter Port, Guernsey) was the husband of Matthew's granddaughter, Mary Morry, and also the business partner of his grandson, John Henry Morry (my 2nd great grandfather). Together, John Henry Morry and Peter Paint Le Messurier purchased the Holdsworth house, lands and waterfront premises from Arthur William Olive Holdsworth in 1844. Both Matthew Morry I and Walter Prideaux were dead and buried by then.

Walter Prideaux was a member of an old and well-respected family in Devon, many of whom, before and after him, were named Walter Prideaux, just to add to the confusion. But this Walter, as it turns out, was a barrister and solicitor, appointed to the High Court of Chancery. He was also a banker, as it happens, though he denied this in several court papers filed during the course of the breakup of his partnership with Matthew Morry I. He denied it because he and one of his banking partners in one of several banks in the South Hams area in which Prideaux was involved directly or indirectly, John Square, were both implicated by Matthew in the fraudulent removal of funds from the reserves of Matthew Morry & Co. as well as the misappropriation of the inheritance Trust of Matthew's grandson, John Foale Morry (all discussed in detail in the next chapter).

According to the Kingsbridge historian Abraham Hawkins:

"A Bank was established at Kingsbridge in the month of February, 1806, by Messrs. Walter Prideaux, John Square, Joseph Hingston, and Walter Prideaux junior. It was first opened in a house on the West side of Fore street nearly opposite the late Buttermarket, and on the North side of Millman's Lane which communicates with the West backlet. An excellent stone mansion however, with an appropriate room for this concern, having been erected by the junior partner on the East side of Fore Street Hill, facing the houses a little above the Quakers' meeting, the business was removed thither in 1808; and, the second partner being dead, but replaced by his son of the same Christian name, and the third removed to Plymouth, where he carries on a similar establishment, the notes of the present firm bear the designation of "Prideaux, Square, and Prideaux," whose Loudon correspondents are messieurs Masterman, Peters, Mildred, & Co. No, 2. White-Hart Court, Gracechurch Street".

Thus, two separate banks involving Walter Prideaux Sr. and his son and grandson were in existence: one at Kingsbridge (Prideaux, Square, and Prideaux) and another at Plymouth (Hingston & Prideaux).

Although this may or may not be relevant to the discussion, Prideaux was also a member of the Society of Friends (Quakers), meaning that by law he could not be forced to swear an oath in

Court, and could therefore not be charged with breaking such an oath by perjuring himself and lying in his testimony.

Figure 31. A Kingsbridge Bank Note[20]

How Matthew came to decide that it would be a good idea to partner with Walter Prideaux is not clear. The court papers presented at the end of the partnership show that Matthew came into the partnership with a number of small fishing vessels to his name, whilst Prideaux supplied additional revenue needed to expand his operations. But Matthew also needed someone he could trust to operate the business in Dartmouth whilst he was the hands-on partner in Newfoundland. And that person needed to have a head on his shoulders because it was his responsibility to keep the books for the company (though Prideaux also denied this in his testimony). Who better than a lawyer, presumably more intelligent and certainly more lettered than Matthew? And quite possibly, for

---

[20] Note the date on this banknote; this was only months or even weeks before the general banking collapse that caused all such "country banks" to go out of business because their holdings were not sufficient to cover the deposits of their clients. The £5 note would have been worthless in a few weeks' time.

it is a common perception, he may have thought that a Quaker would be above any form of dishonest dealings. In this, he was eventually proven wrong. As in any other religion or sect, there are honest, God-fearing adherents, and there are others who are less so.

In any event, the partnership was formed and lasted for approximately thirty-five years, yielding substantial profits for both partners in most years, as court documents also substantiate, before it began to come apart at the seams. And why did it fail? Was it completely because one or both of the partners was bleeding the reserves for his own needs? Court papers support the belief that this was indeed taking place to some extent, and on both sides. Matthew was purchasing property for his own use in Newfoundland out of company funds without the agreement of Prideaux. And Prideaux's banking operations were already beginning to show the signs of strain that caused all of the "country banks", as they were called, to declare insolvency and be terminated during the general banking crash of 1825. So, it is very possible, though not proven, that he was robbing Peter to pay Paul, taking funds from Matthew Morry & Co. to prop up Prideaux, Square & Co. and other banks in which he was a silent partner. However, neither of these questionable practices alone would have led to the cataclysmic failure of a fishing enterprise that had survived and indeed prospered for nearly four decades.

It so happens that this was not the only such fishing enterprise that was suffering a similar fate at this time. And the reason was common to all of them.

In Ronald Rompkey's anthology "Garrison Town to Commercial City – St. John's, Newfoundland, 1800 to 1900" he cites an article in the Colonial Commerce (25-1 1915) which reported that in 1783, after the Treaty of Versailles was signed:

"Many a Newfoundland planter was hopelessly ruined by leaving his money on the books".

Patrick O'Flaherty (Old Newfoundland – a History to 1843) adds:

> "When bread and flour arrived in St. John's from Philadelphia in the summer of 1784, prices immediately fell 30%. Dartmouth merchants responded to the threat posed by cheaper goods from the U.S. by pressing for a total prohibition on American imports, with Holdsworth heading the lobby."

And now those merchants that survived this earlier economic threat were to experience a similar fate in 1815.

O'Flaherty tells us that one of the impacts of the earlier downturn was that:

> "By 1793, the inhabitant fishery was dominant; by 1800, assisted by a war that showed no signs of ending, it had effectively supplanted the fishery from the West Country. (Though a small migratory effort persisted into the next century.)"

This would have spurred Matthew Morry to make more of a solid footing for his business in Newfoundland.

The Napoleonic Wars and the War of 1812 took their toll. W. Gordon Handcock (*English Settlement in Newfoundland*) cites Keith Matthews as indicating that:

> "Between 1789 and 1815, some of the richer merchants [of Dartmouth] (Holdsworth, Teague and Roope) lost commercial interest in Newfoundland, and many others went bankrupt".

It is reported in the Newman Papers (*MG 482 – Newman and Hunt*) at The Rooms that, in 1795 alone, the Americans sank eighty English ships fishing for cod on the Grand Banks and in

Newfoundland waters. But it is an ill wind that blows no good and, the inimitable Judge D. W. Prowse, in his classic book *A History of Newfoundland* reports that, according to Ewen Stabb, a well-known Newfoundland fish merchant working out of Ferryland and St. John's in those days, thirty American prizes were brought into St. John's Harbour at one time, making it possible to walk on the decks of these vessels all the way from Bennett's wharf on the waterfront to Alsop's on the southside. Also, during the hostilities, the French and Americans were excluded from harvesting the cod stocks off Newfoundland, Newfoundland fishing enterprises prospered, and indeed made windfall profits in the monopoly that existed. English merchants, those based solely in England, had all lost interest in the Newfoundland trade due to increased competition for a somewhat diminished resource, having made their fortunes in the 17th and 18th centuries and were no longer a force to be reckoned with. The Newfoundland Historical Society's little book, *A Short History of Newfoundland and Labrador*, gives a slightly different explanation for the loss of interest:

> *"The British migratory fishery at Newfoundland had already been traumatized by a massive production of fish in 1788 – more fish than the markets in Europe could absorb. Prices had collapsed and a series of bankruptcies rippled through the trade."*

Martin Wilcox (*Fishing and Fishermen – a Guide for Family Historians*) suggests that it was, in fact, the prolonged conflict with France after 1793 that was instrumental in bringing to an end the British involvement in the Newfoundland fishery. But he goes on to say:

> *"Another reason for the British withdrawal from the Newfoundland [fishery] was that developments nearer home were making such a distant and risky business unnecessary.*

The white fisheries [groundfish like haddock and cod] in the late eighteenth century, hitherto second to herring in importance, underwent a series of major developments that laid the foundations for their rapid development in the nineteenth century."

But, whatever the root causes of the British withdrawal from Newfoundland may have been, the minute that these wars were over and the peace treaties signed, the fishing fleets of France and the USA returned to the banks and the bottom fell out of the salt cod market overnight. It is reported in a number of the histories of that time that wholesale prices for salt cod dropped to one half of their former value overnight. And fortunes that had been established in large part by legally taking French and American vessels as prizes were now eliminated. Matthew Morry and Company suffered as a result of both of these factors, having enjoyed the windfall profits when they existed, and having failed to see the end when it was in sight and take measures to stave off financial ruin by tightening their belts.

Matthew Morry & Co. had not only made money by taking foreign prizes, but it had also lost money from the reverse also occurring. A 28-page document (*D1187 - Contested Cause - Captured Ship Dorsetshire Master Morry*) from the National Archives (Kew) pertaining to a contestation of the ownership of the cargo on board a vessel named the DORSETSHIRE in 1804 tells this tale. This vessel had been taken as a Prize by the French privateer, SORCIÉRE, and then recaptured by the Royal Navy vessel MOUCHERON (obviously captured from the French also, given its name). The Commander of the DORSETSHIRE was named Richard Morry (note the spelling) and he testified that the vessel was owned by Matthew Morry and Walter Prideaux. This Richard Morry could be none other than the Richard Morrey, as I have him and as Margaret Dickson had him. He was known to be a Master Mariner and no other man with a similar name in

Dartmouth existed at the time at an age suitable to be this person. Since the vessel was captured by a Royal Naval vessel in the hands of a French crew attempting to return it to France for either a bounty or for sale, when the vessel was recaptured by the Royal Navy it became the property of the Crown, with the naval vessel's captain and crew entitled to a portion of the Prize money. Both Matthew Morry and Company and the owner of the cargo, a man named Lyme from Portsmouth, filed a claim for return of these goods and the vessel. As is frustratingly normal for the court cases at the Archives, the decision, in this case, is not contained in the files. Note that Richard Morry/Morrey and Matthew Morry were 1st cousins.

There is an even sadder denouement to the story of the DORSETSHIRE recounted above. In 2018, I discovered on a website known as FindMyPast a list of English prisoners of war captured by the French during the Napoleonic wars who died in captivity. Richard Morry or Morrey's name appeared on that list. He died in a French prison on Nov. 19, 1805, one year after the capture of his vessel, the DORSETSHIRE. A number of other family members spent time (sometimes years) in French prisons during these conflicts, but this was the first time I have seen evidence of one of them dying as a result of the dreadful conditions in those prisons or the wounds they sustained in their capture.

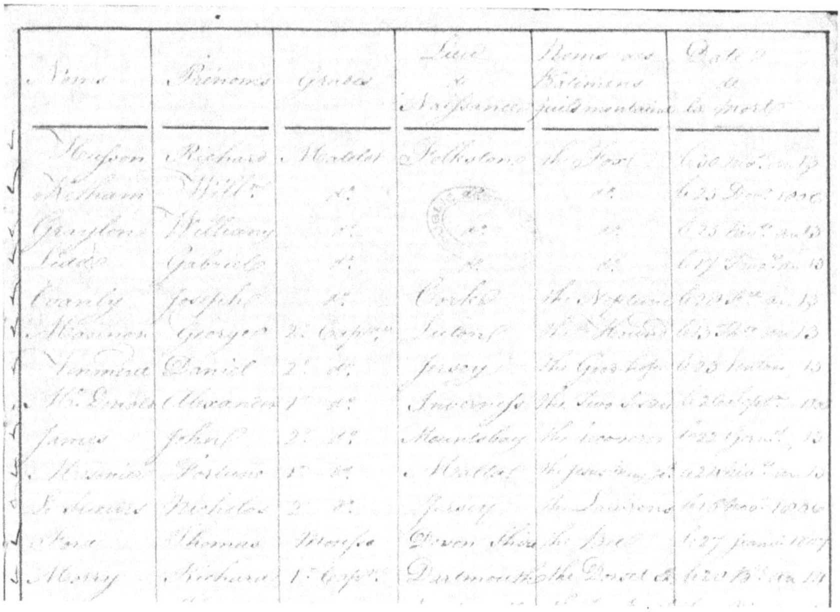

Figure 32. Death of Richard Morry as French Prisoner of War

One last piece of information concerning Matthew's family in Dartmouth that recently (2017) came to light is worthy of mention.

While visiting the Devon Archives at the Southwest Heritage Trust in Exeter, I came upon a series of microfiche cards that contained images of the pages of the Dartmouth Borough Tax Assessments, 1747-1832. Not having the time to explore all of these in detail on this visit, I examined one for the year 1750, the year Matthew Morry I was born, and then skipped to the 1780s and later, when his career would have been taking off. In the 1750 accounts, there are a number of entries of people with a name similar to Morry renting properties and paying small amounts of taxes on the rent. There is also a reference to the officers of the Borough, the money they earned and the taxes they paid on their salaries. Here we find an apparent reference to the salary being made by Matthew's father, John, as Tidesman/Boatsman (a government appointment as Customs Collector for the Port of Dartmouth), - £30 4S and 10P – on which he paid taxes of £4 10S.

On the microfiche covering the later period after 1780, I was surprised to find that Matthew Morry and indeed his brother-in-law, Christopher Graham, who were both ship's Masters and also a shipowner, in Matthew's case at least, were not the owners of their properties in Dartmouth but rather were renters. And it would appear from the assessments that the premises of Christopher Graham must have been more commodious, if not more luxurious, than those of Matthew and his family. Interestingly, Matthew is renting his premises from Robert Holdsworth and, though there is no mention of the location, it is known that the Holdsworths owned Mount Boone, a very prestigious property on Crowther's Hill, the height of land overlooking Dartmouth Harbour, and it may be that they were renting a building associated with that property to Matthew. Many other Morrys were also found in these tax assessments, all as renters, not owners.

CHAPTER SEVEN – COURT CASES INVOLVING MATTHEW AND JOHN MORRY

"This chapter will be of no use to lawyers and of no interest to others" [21]

Introduction

It is necessary to take a pause here in the chronology of our narrative to discuss in some detail, but by no means the level of detail possible, the many court cases in England and Newfoundland that have served as such a rich source of personal

---

[21] With apologies to the great Will Durant, who said this of his chapter on Roman Law in *Caesar and Christ*, Volume III of his opus work, *The Story of Civilization*. His self-effacing, self-mocking comment was untrue, and I fervently hope that the reader will also come to the same judgement of this chapter.

information on Matthew Morry I, and to a lesser extent his sons, John and Thomas Graham, and also his grandson, John Foale Morry. These cases spanned a period of more than a decade from 1813 to 1824 and probably there were vestiges of them remaining to be resolved after that time.

For those interested in seeing greater detail, the full account of these fascinating court cases has been prepared as a chapter to be published by the *S. S. Daisy* Legal-History Committee of The Law Society of Newfoundland and Labrador in Volume III of *A Ferryland Merchant-Magistrate – The Journal and Cases of Robert Carter, J. P.*

As an aside, the Robert Carter, J. P. referenced above was a member of the established family of merchants in Ferryland at the time of the arrival of Matthew Morry I. It was Robert Carter Senior, the grandfather of the Journalist mentioned, who actually assisted Matthew in obtaining his first grant of waterside property in Caplin Bay by putting in a good word for him with the Governor. His word was that influential because he had played a major role more than once in arming the local citizenry and fending off attacks by the French, not only in Ferryland but in St. John's. Moreover, it was Anne, the daughter of Robert Carter Senior and the aunt of Robert Carter, J. P., who became the second wife of Matthew Morry after his permanent relocation to Newfoundland from Devon.

Matthew Morry's presence in the English Court system was associated with two different but related events; the death of his son, John, the Privateer, and associated matters related to the inheritance that John left to his only child, John Foale Morry; and the final rancorous and drawn out Court battles over the demise of Matthew's partnership with Walter Prideaux in Matthew Morry & Co. His presence in the Newfoundland Court system was also related to the latter issue, though there are legal documents – indentures and the like – found in the papers of various Courts in

Newfoundland that pertain to the issues surrounding the inheritance of John Foale Morry as well.

In an attempt to simplify these discussions, I will separate these related court cases from one another by dealing with them according to the Court system within which the cases were heard. A tabulation of the 13 court cases can be found in Appendix 3 in specific enough references for any reader interested to find the original court documents in the National Archives in England and the Provincial Archives in Newfoundland.

His Majesty's High Court of Chancery

Most of the cases heard in England that pertain to Matthew Morry were heard in His Majesty's High Court of Chancery. This Court system, which no longer exists in England, was in place for centuries because the Courts of Common Law did not always allow a fair hearing for certain kinds of challenges, those referred to as "equity" cases, often consisting of a contentious family or business matter.

1. Morry v Rowe: C 13/1987/62. 3rd July 1811.

Plaintiff: Matthew Morry. *Defendant:* Joshua Rowe.

Bill only.

Matthew Morry's firstborn son, John, was a Privateer, Master of the Ship of War, the ALEXANDER, holding Letters of Marque from the Crown. He died sometime in February of 1807, as did his younger brother Thomas Graham. The evidence is circumstantial, but in the absence of burial records for either man in Dartmouth, it seems likely they died together in a battle with a foreign vessel they were attempting to capture.

At the time of John's death, numerous newspaper advertisements have been found pertaining to the auction of various prizes he had captured. One of the auctioneers responsible was a man from Cornwall named Joshua Rowe. It appears from the details of this "Bill" (complaint before the Court) that Rowe never did deliver to Matthew Morry, as the executor of his son's estate, his share of the proceeds of the sale of one captured vessel. Note that this was only one of several prizes captured by John that were up for auction at the time of his death or soon afterwards.

The outcome of this case is unknown. This is unfortunately too typical of the court cases found in the National Archives. The final judgements were seldom recorded and are nowhere to be found. But from the financial details given in several of the cases below, Matthew never declared that any income from this or any other prize auction was received into the estate of his late son. We can take this for what it is worth. It seems unlikely that all the auctioneers defaulted in their duty. It seems more plausible that the funds were indeed paid to Matthew as executor but never deposited into the trust for his grandson, John Foale Morry. We can therefore only imagine what became of them.

2. Morry v Newman: C 13/2148/31. 30th June 1819.

Plaintiff: Matthew Morry. Defendants: Robert Newman, Walter Prideaux, Walter Were Prideaux and Robert Were Prideaux.

Bill and Answer.

I am presenting these cases in the order in which they appear in the court records in the National Archives. Often cases are presented out of chronological or even logical order if there were two or more related cases being heard during the same era. Such is the case here.

The defendant, in this case, Robert Newman, was a well-known shipbuilder in Dartmouth. Matthew Morry & Co. had a longstanding relationship with this man's shipyard for the construction and repair of their vessels. But when the partnership between Mathew Morry and Walter Prideaux began to fall apart in 1813, some strange events took place involving Robert Newman, which Matthew contended were orchestrated by his ex-partner, Prideaux, to defraud him of his fair share of the assets of the partnership at dissolution. He contended that after an earlier bankruptcy Newman had fallen in debt to one of the banks operated by Prideaux and his relatives and partners and could thus be pressured into doing Prideaux's bidding.

Newman billed Matthew Morry & Company for repairs to the Brig PRISCILLA, one of the vessels owned by the company. Matthew insisted the bills had already been paid and this case was taken out to prevent that bill from being paid out of the remaining assets of the company.

Once again, we are completely in the dark as to the outcome of this court case. But combined with the details presented in other related cases below it looks like Matthew was not successful.

3. Morry v Newman: C 13/2148/32. 30th June 1819.

Plaintiff: Matthew Morry. Defendants: Robert Newman, Walter Prideaux, Walter Were Prideaux and Robert Were Prideaux.

Bill and Answer.

Another Bill on the same date and involving the same players concerns a somewhat different matter.

Once again, Newman has charged the company an even larger amount for other repairs to the PRISCILLA at another time which again Matthew contends had been paid for.

Evidence is presented that Prideaux had (fraudulently and clandestinely?) transferred his share of ownership of this and other vessels to two grandsons named in the Bill and that they were largely responsible for having Newman seize the vessel and prevent Matthew from taking it back to Newfoundland with him.

Matthew was thereby deprived of the means of carrying on his livelihood, in addition to being stuck with the (fraudulent) bill for work orders he contended had already been paid.

It is important to note at this juncture that, in all of these related cases, it was made clear that Matthew was not keeping a set of day books for all related business expenses, instead relying on Prideaux to keep detailed records. Prideaux states on more than one occasion that it was Morry's responsibility to keep such records and hence refuses to allow him access to the books he himself had been keeping for the entire 35+ years that the partnership existed. So, Matthew does appear to be at least in part to blame for the situation in which he finds himself and really cannot prove one way or the other which bills had been paid and which had not.

To add insult to injury, Newman later presented an even larger bill to the company for dry-dock storage of the PRISCILLA that was not ordered by Matthew but rather by Prideaux's grandsons to keep the vessel out of Matthew's hands.

Again, the outcome of the case can only be guessed.

4. Morry v Hunt: C 13/2148/39. 30th April 1819.

Plaintiff: John Morry. Defendants: Walter Prideaux, Matthew Morry and William Cholwich Hunt.

Bill and Three Answers.

This is the first of several complaints lodged by John Foale Morry against his own grandfather, Matthew Morry, and others who had various levels of legal obligation to properly manage the trust that had been left to him following the deaths of his parents in 1807. At the time of this complaint, John was still a minor, or "infant" in the terminology of the Court and had to be represented by a "next friend" who, in this case, turned out to be Dr. Nicholas Brand, an Exeter man who had spent time in Ferryland in the late 1700s and early 1800s and was well familiar with Matthew Morry.

I am at odds over whether or not Matthew was actually working behind the scenes with John and Nicholas and whether the real targets of this suit may have been Prideaux and the other man named, William Cholwich Hunt. The latter had been named as a trustee of the estate but clearly, he made no financial gain from it and later any charges against him were dismissed outright. But evidence does exist that Prideaux had a lot to do with the virtually total misappropriation of the trust funds, with or without the collusion of Matthew, for each man's personal benefit, as well as for the benefit of their partnership. For example, the evidence presented shows that some of John Foale Morry's trust had been used to pay the funerary expenses of not only his father and mother but even his uncle, Thomas Graham Morry. This was surely not an appropriate charge against those funds. Similarly, large portions of the trust funds intended to pay for John's care and maintenance were used to pay large bills owed by Prideaux without any explanation of why this should be considered appropriate.

An interesting fact emerges in this case material that figures in most, if not all, of the related cases. Walter Prideaux was a Barrister and Solicitor and hence an officer of the very Court in which the cases were being heard. Moreover, he was an upstanding figure in the society of Dartmouth with many influential friends, unlike Matthew Morry. Hence, when it came time to appoint Commissioners to take testimony and render their opinions to the Judge in the case, the names of these Commissioners, selected from amongst the cream of Dartmouth Society, invariably included friends, relatives and business partners of Prideaux. In this case, those named were Nicholas Brooking the younger, Thomas Harris, William Were Prideaux and John Doe, Gentlemen. Nicholas Brooking Jr. was Walter Prideaux's partner in his law practice and, as we have seen above, William Were Prideaux was another of his grandsons. I cannot say what relationship the other two men may have had with him but this information is sufficient to determine that Matthew had the deck stacked against him.

The outcome of this case and several related ones which follow was dragged out for several years, but it does appear that somehow John was vindicated and the two men, his grandfather and his grandfather's partner, who benefited most from his trust were made to reimburse him, at least in part.

5. Morry v Prideaux: C 13/2350/8. 2nd June 1820.

Plaintiff: John Morry. *Defendants:* Walter Prideaux, Matthew Morry and William Cholwich Hunt.

Two Interrogatories and three Depositions

This case followed on directly from the one above. In point of fact, C 13/2350/8 is two cases combined into one by the Court, since they pertain to much the same matters.

The crux of this combined case was to delve into whatever became of the so-called £3 Per Cent Annuities left by John Morry in the first instance to his widow, but which were then quickly to be added to the trust for their son, John Foale Morry, because she died almost immediately after her husband, leaving their seven-year-old son, John, an orphan in his grandfather's care.

Several witnesses were called to testify in this matter. From their testimony it is impossible not to come to the conclusion that Prideaux connived to trick his business partner, Matthew Morry, who was a Trustee of the estate, to allow these government bonds to be sold and to have the profits used for a variety of purposes, none of which were to the benefit of the intended recipient, John Foale Morry. I cannot conclude that Matthew Morry was blameless in this. He may not have had legal training but he must have recognised that the end use of these funds for the benefit of Prideaux, Matthew Morry & Co. and Matthew himself could in no way be construed to be legal and correct.

6. Morry v Prideaux: C 13/1441/6. 22nd December 1820.

Plaintiff: John Morry. Defendants: Matthew Morry and Walter Prideaux.

Two sets of Depositions

Despite the notations above, there was a third defendant that John Foale Morry believed was complicit in the misappropriation of the funds that were realised from the sale of the £3 Per Cent Annuities in his Trust Fund – John Square. This name is important, as we shall soon see. He was Walter Prideaux's partner in a banking enterprise in Kingsbridge and that bank played a key role in the dispersal of the funds to Prideaux, Matthew Morry and Matthew Morry & Co. that were intended to have been reinvested in real estate. As we shall also see, John Square was also the person who brought charges against Matthew Morry & Co. in Newfoundland, almost certainly at the behest of Walter Prideaux in order to seize the assets of the failed partnership in that country. Therefore, the omission of his name from the list of defendants in the caption above is a serious oversight by either the Court itself or the National Archives when they filed the document.

In response to this "Cause" brought forward by John Foale Morry, Matthew Morry was acting only in his own defence, as there was no longer any relationship between him and Prideaux and the third Defendant, John Square, was clearly in Prideaux's corner. But in the documents filed with the Court, we only see the depositions of five friends of Prideaux giving evidence on his behalf. Similar documents for Matthew and for John Square, if they ever existed, have been lost. This is not at all uncommon with such files at the National Archives. They are almost never complete. The five depositions essentially cast mud at Matthew

Morry implying he was dipping into the cookie jar on his own and making free with the partnership's funds and resources. Since this had nothing to do with the complaint raised by John Foale Morry (he was only concerned with the loss of his own inheritance, not the funds belonging to the partnership, of which he had no interest), a proper Court of Law would have disallowed this testimony. It was clearly only elicited by Prideaux to further his own ends in the cases involving he and Matthew Morry specifically.

This was another of the cases which dragged on for several years – five in fact, from 1820 to 1825. Every few months the Court issued one of their "Decrees and Orders" to attempt to move the process along but every time foot-dragging by Prideaux and his lawyer delayed the outcome that much longer. A final Decree and Order was issued on July 26th, 1825 requiring Walter Prideaux and Matthew Morry, each in his own right and to a greater or lesser extent according to calculations done by the "Master" appointed by the Court, to make restitution to John Foale Morry. However, the Master's calculations made significant reductions in the amounts to be repaid by Prideaux on flimsy and non-credible excuses. For example, Prideaux was able to persuade the Master that he was owed £300 for certain goods and services ostensibly but questionably provided to John Foale Morry. However, the Master augmented that deduction from the amount of his repayment due to the Trust fund by another amount almost as large for interest on the original sum. No such measures were taken to diminish the amount Matthew was to pay his grandson. Perhaps that was only fair. But the treatment the two "co-conspirators" received was far from equal, especially considering that the evidence suggested that Prideaux was in reality far more culpable than Matthew Morry.

7. Morry v Prideaux: C 13/2155/2 1818-1819.

Plaintiff: Matthew Morry. Defendants: Walter Prideaux and John Square.

Two Bills and One Answer

    This is the last case that exists in the files of His Majesty's High Court of Chancery that is still in existence and accessible at the National Archives in Kew. It is probably the most important case file of all the court case files to be found in England or in Newfoundland because it includes (though not stated in the summary above) an appendix attached representing the financial books of the entire history of the partnership for some thirty plus years. The appendix alone fills 29 large sized sheepskins. More information is contained here on the partnership than in all other sources available, though how credible this information may be is open to judgement. For example, the appendix is comprised of financial records which were compiled by Walter Prideaux and in the completion of which Matthew Morry played no part. We can, therefore, surmise that these "facts" will have been carefully laid out to support the allegations made by Walter Prideaux and his banking partner, John Square.

    In the simplest of terms, this case was brought by Matthew Morry against Walter Prideaux and John Square because (as we shall see below) they had conspired to take legal action against him in both the Court of King's Bench in England and the Supreme Court in Newfoundland which, if fully successful, would bankrupt and ruin him. We do not know the outcome of the case before the Court of King's Bench, because no record of it can be found at the National Archives where it should be available. However, we do know that John Square was successful in convincing the Supreme

Court of Newfoundland in St. John's that Matthew Morry was heavily indebted to him, and he was given authorisation to seize and sell much of Matthew Morry's property in Newfoundland whilst Matthew was in England defending himself against other legal challenges by Walter Prideaux and Robert Newman, as well as his own grandson, John Foale Morry.

Unfortunately, despite the remarkable amount of information accompanying this Pleading, this is just one more of many Chancery cases for which an outcome or judgement cannot be found.

His Majesty's Court of King's Bench

At the time that these cases were being heard, the Court of King's Bench was divided into two parts – the Crown Side, for criminal charges brought by the government against a citizen; and the Plea Side, for lawsuits between two citizens. The Court in which the following cases were heard was the Plea Side. To the best of my knowledge, no criminal charges were ever levelled against any of the participants in these affairs.

From his testimony in the High Court of Chancery above, we know that Matthew Morry was being sued in the Court of King's Bench by both Robert Newman and John Square, or at least he believed that these cases were to be lodged against him there. As it turns out, there is no evidence of a case by John Square in the records available at the National Archives. If such a case existed, the record of it has been entirely lost. This is not common. Usually, some vestige remains. My feeling is that Walter Prideaux and John Square misled Matthew Morry into believing that they were going to sue him in the Court of King's Bench but, realising that the case could go against them, they had second thoughts and did not file it.

There were also two other cases found that involved either Matthew Morry or Walter Prideaux but I will reserve discussion on them until they are briefly presented below.

1. KB 122-1002-1762, 1818

Prideaux and Prideaux vs Prideaux and Morry

This is one of the two cases not mentioned by Matthew Morry in his testimony in the High Court of Chancery. Here we have the grandsons of Walter Prideaux, Walter Were Prideaux and Robert Were Prideaux who were ostensibly gifted their grandfather's share of the Brig PRISCILLA suing Matthew Morry & Company, that is their own grandfather and his former partner, Matthew Morry for money they claim they expended equipping a vessel for a voyage to Caplin Bay.

Once again, the two former partners are not even talking to one another anymore, let alone cooperating with one another in responding to such a charge. Instead, Prideaux adopts a legal ploy which is identical to one he is seen using in another case, an insurance claim brought against Matthew Morry & Co. before the Guild Hall in London (see the case immediately following this one). He pleads guilty, leaving Matthew to contest what is more than likely a fabricated charge. If Matthew loses, the Court will take settlement from him first and foremost and only if he is unable to satisfy the full amount of the claim will the Court assess the remainder against Prideaux. And of course, we can surmise that his grandsons would then magnanimously forgive his share of the "debt". In the case before the Guild Hall, the Judge smelled a rat and dismissed the case. We do not know if the same occurred here because once again the Judgement is missing from the file.

2. KB 122-1011-1690, 1819

Britten & Olive vs Morry & Prideaux

As stated above, this case is almost a perfect parallel to the one brought against Matthew Morry & Co. by Walter Prideaux's grandsons. Britten and Olive charge that they are owed a large amount of money for insurance charges owed on an earlier voyage of a vessel owned by the company. Walter Prideaux again pleads guilty, leaving Matthew Morry to fight the once again very obvious trumped up charge. As previously observed, this tactic would have ensured that, if Matthew had been found guilty, he would have been made to pay the damages first and foremost, and only that portion which he was unable to pay would be charged against Prideaux.

The Judge detected that the lawyer for the Complainants is John Square, Walter Prideaux's banking and legal partner, and that he had never before worked for these Complainants. Square also presented all the supporting documents for the claim, which did not originate with the Complainants but rather with Prideaux. Seeing this for what it was, a clear-cut case of collusion between Prideaux and the Complainants, the Judge instructed the Jury accordingly and they dismissed all the charges.

3. KB 122-1020-2914, 1819

Newman vs Morry & Prideaux

This case did not go so smoothly for Matthew Morry. Although it was ostensibly being brought against the two partners of Matthew Morry & Co. to settle a charge against that company for work on their vessels by Robert Newman, this has all the appearances of being another collusion between Prideaux and Newman. The same tactic was employed here by Prideaux whereby he did not contest the Cause.

Judgement was recorded in this instance and it went against Matthew Morry & Co. The Sheriff of Devonshire exacted as much as he could by the sale of Matthew Morry's property in England and then contended that he could not locate Walter Prideaux in order to exact the remaining damages. This, of course, is patently absurd. This is a pillar of Devon society with several properties all over the county as well as several businesses, including his law practice and a number of banks in which he held an interest.

4. KB 122-1033-781, 1820

Graham et al vs Prideaux

There is one other case I found in the files of the Court of King's Bench which did not involve Matthew Morry but caught my eye because it did involve Walter Prideaux and one other familiar name, Graham.

Matthew Morry's sisters-in-law, Jennet Graham, Sarah Clift and Elizabeth Ellis were acting as the Executrixes of the estate of their late mother, Mary [Churchwill] Graham, Matthew's mother-in-law. They brought this case against Walter Prideaux because they believed he owed their mother a good deal of money at the time of her death. She owned several businesses and property around Devon, acquired most likely to earn a living after her husband, Christopher Graham, had died.

Prideaux's counter-argument was that Mary Graham owed him greater sums of money than those claimed in the suit were owed by him to Mary Graham. This was a typical ploy for Prideaux, turning around the charges against him and making the opposite charges, only more so.

Unfortunately, once again there is no conclusion to this case and we do not know whose position was vindicated. But it fits a pattern that Walter Prideaux was feeling the financial pinch in the latter years of his partnership with Matthew Morry, very likely because of the fact that the banks in which he was a principal were also beginning to fail at that time and needed infusions of funds to remain solvent.

The Supreme Court of Newfoundland

There are only two court cases found in the annals of the Supreme Court of Newfoundland and its subsidiary Surrogate Court of the Southern District in Ferryland pertaining to the above English cases, though indeed there were numerous other trivial cases involving Matthew Morry I or II, mainly pertaining to matters in dispute over the wages of employees, minor land-related disputes and the like.

1. Square v Matthew Morry & Co - GN 5-2-A-1

Supreme Court Central Minutes Box 28. 14 Sept. 1818

In the midst of all of the actions described above taking place in England, and with Matthew spending his time in Devon and London defending himself against this blizzard of court actions, while simultaneously seeking injunctions and dismissal of these cases through actions he himself initiated before the High Court of Chancery, John Square sneaked off to St. John's and put his case before the Supreme Court of Newfoundland.

The records of the Supreme Court held at The Rooms in St. John's are not the rigid legal documents that we see in the collections of the Court of King's Bench and High Court of Chancery documents at Kew in England. There are pluses and minuses in that distinction. Certainly, the Court records held at the Provincial Archives Division are easier to understand, being written in layman's English, not legalese. And they even give some important insights into what the trial Judge (unnamed) was thinking as he heard and passed Judgement in the case. And indeed, a Judgement is to be found, unlike in the vast majority of cases heard in the English Courts. That is very useful. But, on the other hand, we lose a great deal of the detail of the original submissions from Plaintiff and Defendant that provide their own insights, though obviously they must be treated with the understanding of their being written in a very biased manner.

One supporting piece of information provided by Square to substantiate his personal claim to the assets of Matthew Morry & Company has recently come to light. As in the National Archives in England, the Provincial Archives of Newfoundland and Labrador do not always retain all elements of a court case in one place it seems. Quite apart from the Supreme Court Central Minutes mentioned above, there is a collection of documents loosely known as "GN 169 - Miscellaneous Deeds and Wills, 1744-1859 - 22 Volumes" that does, as its name implies, contain hundreds of unrelated deeds, wills and other legal documents associated with the business of various Courts in St. John's during the years mentioned. One of them, it turns out, is a copy of an Indenture between Walter Prideaux and John Square, made out on August 12, 1816 in England, by which Prideaux effectively sold or "leased" his half share interest in the properties of Matthew Morry & Company in Caplin Bay for the sum of £800. It must be assumed that the reason that this copy of the Indenture exists in the Newfoundland court records is that it was presented by Square at the time of this court case as supporting evidence. The date of this document is important. It coincides precisely with the timing of Matthew Morry's first attempts to have the partnership with Prideaux dissolved. And thus, it indicates that Prideaux and Square were already scheming two years before Square presented his case before the Newfoundland Supreme Court to provide justification for Square seizing the assets of the company in Newfoundland.

Overall, the conclusion of the Justice of the Supreme Court was that, even though John Square's affidavits and testimony were not credible, Matthew Morry's solicitor did nothing to refute them, and thus, in the end, the Judge had little recourse other than to rule in favour of the Plaintiff. With the result that much of Matthew Morry's property in Caplin Bay was ordered seized and sold to pay what may very well have been a fallacious debt.

However....

The matter did not end there (it seems none of these court cases ever really ended!). Shortly after the order was given by the Supreme Court in St. John's for the property of Matthew Morry & Co. to be seized to satisfy John Square's claim, a sort of restraining order was sought by Matthew Morry's solicitor, his son Matthew Morry II, in the Supreme Court, Southern District, in Ferryland.

2. J. Square vs M. Morry & Co - GN 5 1 C 1 52-54

30 Sept. 1818

Commission on the Case of John Square V Mathw. Morry & Co.

The preamble to the Court record in this matter reads:

> "Whereas Mathew [sic] Morry & Company of Caplin Bay in the district of Ferryland Merchants have Appealed to his Majesty in Council from A Judgement obtained against them in the Supreme Court of the Said Island at the Suit of John Square___"

This, in and of itself, gives an inkling of the ease with which the Courts in Newfoundland could be deceived with incorrect or insufficient information in cases such as these since it was too difficult and time-consuming to await the corroboration of the facts from England. In point of fact, one of the main arguments that Matthew Morry I gave in support of his cases being heard before the High Court of Equity in England was precisely that he would not be able to challenge the decision of the Supreme Court of Newfoundland to His Majesty in Council. The reason is quite simple: The Crown had long ago decided it would not meddle in the affairs of Newfoundland by entertaining appeals against the decisions of the Supreme Court of Newfoundland.

The Order being given here by the Chief Justice of Newfoundland, Frances Forbes, Esq., to the Stipendiary Magistrate of the Surrogate Court in Ferryland, Robert Carter (Matthew Morry's nephew by marriage, as it happens) was blatantly false and the Chief Justice undoubtedly knew this point of law very well and was under no illusions in this regard. Unlike Stipendiary Magistrates, the Chief Justice had training in the law and would have certainly known that Matthew could not appeal his judgement to the Crown. Yet he issued this restraining order despite that. The Chief Justice had already indicated in the case brought by John Square that he doubted the credibility of the affidavits Square presented in support of his contention that he was owed this money. Apparently, the Chief Justice also doubted John Square's contention that the Court of King's Bench was about to, or already had, given him leave to seize the property of Matthew Morry and Company in Newfoundland. Yet even though the Chief Justice had noted that Matthew Morry's lawyer had not sufficiently refuted these claims, the Chief Justice effectively issued a restraining order against the carrying out of his own judgement! It may be judged that Matthew Morry enjoyed as much favour (bias?) in the Newfoundland Court system as Walter Prideaux and his partners did in the English Court system.

As with almost all the other cases above, in Courts in England and Newfoundland, we have no idea how this panned out in the end. However, we do know that Matthew Morry II and his descendants continued to operate the business affairs of the family in Caplin Bay and Ferryland for many years to come. As for the founder of the dynasty, Matthew Morry I, he was now almost seventy years of age and probably quite content to allow the younger generations to fight these battles for him in future.

Figure 33. A "Complaint" Filed with High Court of Chancery

Dimensions roughly 1 metre on a side

Questions and Answers Concerning Court Records

To summarise this account of Matthew Morry's (and, by extension, John Foale Morry's) court records, a Q&A is provided below in which the questions seem obvious from the above but the answers are but one subjective response to those questions. Each reader can reach his or her own conclusions.

1. Was Matthew Morry a crook?

Or was he a dupe to a sharp lawyer and business partner?

Or was he simply a lousy businessman?

In my opinion, he was all and none of the above. He more than likely did take more out of the business partnership resources than he ought to have had as the annual income began to decline to satisfy the living expenses of his family in the style to which they had become accustomed. But so too did Walter Prideaux, in his case to prop up his other failing partnerships in banking. Also, they both certainly did misuse the resources in John Foale Morry's inheritance trust, but it seems likely that Matthew Morry was less culpably guilty in that case than his lawyer business partner who knew what he was doing was illegal. Matthew most probably assumed that he had a right to those funds since he was the executor of the estate and was providing for the living expenses and education of his grandson. I do believe that Matthew Morry was a poor businessman, in that he failed to keep adequate daybook accounts of his part of the business transactions and hence had no idea of the deteriorating state of the company's accounts. On the other hand, Walter Prideaux did keep accurate accounts and evidently kept Matthew in the dark as things began to decline, while at the same time probably continuing to bleed the accounts himself. Thus, it does seem likely that Matthew was duped to some extent by an unscrupulous business partner.

2. Did this lead to his leaving England forever?

Indirectly, the answer seems to me to be yes. From his testimony in Court, he stated that he was in the process of preparing to retire to England when the company finances exploded. After these court cases his personal property in England had all been seized by the Court to pay off real or fraudulently claimed debts. In addition, due to his not being of the same social status in Dartmouth as Prideaux, what reputation he had there would have been ruined as a result of this war with Prideaux. So, in the end, he was left with no alternative than to move outright to Newfoundland to live with his son and grandchildren. By this time, the court records make clear that Matthew was married to Anne [née Carter], so we must assume that the two of them intended to retire to England together. If this is a fair analysis, then Matthew's reasons for staying in Newfoundland had less to do with the better prospects for making a living there, which likely motivate the majority of the small-scale West Country merchant class, of which he was a member, and more a matter of necessity and desperation.

3. Did Matthew and his Grandson ever reconcile?

All that can be said with certainty based on the evidence is that Matthew did return some, if not all, of the funds he had taken from John's Trust, that they both continued to work together out of Caplin Bay and, most importantly, when John died the year after his grandfather, he was buried with Matthew and they share a common headstone. Whether Matthew dictated this latter course is not known. But it does appear that the two men either never had a falling out (their opposition in Court may have been more apparent than real, intended to corner the real culpable party, Walter Prideaux) or they were able to restore amicable relations after the Courts had rendered justice in some measure for John.

4. Did Matthew Morry ever receive any Justice?

Not directly. He was no match for the legal machinations of his partner, and the court cases mounted directly or indirectly by Prideaux nominally against Matthew Morry & Co. but really aimed at his former partner apparently went against Matthew almost exclusively, so far as we can tell from the court records.

I did discover one passing reference to the denouement of Matthew Morry's travails with John Square and "one other", whom I take to be Walter Prideaux. I found this brief entry in a place I would rather not have found it, a publication of the British Privy Council entitled *"Slave Trade – Three Volumes, Session 21 November 1826 – 2 July 1827"*. This large volume contains almost exclusively information pertaining to the slave trade, but at the very back there is a nine-page appendix entitled: *"Appeals from the Colonies"* which appears to have been added to the volume almost as an afterthought, and which seems to only belong here because the Appeals in question were made by individuals in the Colonies against judgements in England apparently. At least, I fervently hope that these pages have nothing to do with the subject matter of the remainder of this large volume.

The sole entry here of pertinence reads:

"Newfoundland – Matthew Morry vs. John Square & another, Petition of Appeal lodged 2 June [year not given], disposed of 10 March 1824 – Judgement affirmed on regular hearing."

This would seem to indicate that Matthew Morry had filed an appeal against the judgement in the case of John Square and Walter Prideaux, the appeal had gone against him, and the judgement was upheld upon a hearing at the Privy Council.

Justice denied? Perhaps. On the other hand, it must have been some satisfaction to Matthew, in the sense of the German *schadenfreude*[22], to be able to observe from a distance the ultimate failure of all of Walter Prideaux and his family's banking enterprises during the crash of the Country Banks in 1825-26.

---

[22] Pleasure derived by someone from another person's misfortune.

APPEAL FROM THE COLONIES

1819. Names of the COLONIES.	NAMES of the PARTIES.	PETITION OF APPEAL		COMPROMISED. Or otherwise disposed of.
		When lodged.	When disposed of.	
Newfoundland	Hutchins vs. Stewart,	22 January	10 Feb. 1819	Dismissed for non-prosecution.
St. Vincent's	John Grant vs. Alexander Cumming,	27 January		
Jamaica	Robert Wilton & another vs. John Mason & Us.	24 February	9 June 1821	Judgment affirmed on regular hearing.
Demerara	Michael Sutton vs. Benj. Fayle & James Swanzy,	10 March		
The Cape of Good Hope	Geo. March & Thos. Charles Cadogan vs. Abraham Faux & another,	5 March	28 May 1819	Dismissed for non-prosecution.
Jamaica	James Barrett Virgo, esq. vs. Walton Mirzo, esq. & others,	10 April	30 June 1821	
St. Vincent's	Daniel Henry Rucker & others vs. Charles Grant,	3 May	31 Jan. 1824	
Isle of Man	Patrick Carron vs. John Walker & others,	6 May	19 June 1819	Dismissed for non-prosecution.
Jamaica	John Cross Rose vs. Alexander Edgar,	11 May	9 June 1821	Judgment affirmed as regular hearing.
Jamaica	William Marshall Clerk & others vs. William M'Dowall,	11 May	10 Oct. 1820	Appeal withdrawn by consent.
Newfoundland	Matthew Morry vs. John Square & another,	2 June	10 Mar. 1824	Judgment affirmed on regular hearing.
Bengal (Suddy Dewanny Adaulut)	Neelhont Biswas vs. Rajah Mutterjeet Sing,	14 June		Dismissed for non-prosecution.
Jamaica	John Wateridge vs. William Hall, esq.	9 July	18 May 1822	Judgment affirmed on regular hearing.
Jersey	P. Perrott vs. Dean of Jersey,	16 July		
D°	Dean of Jersey vs. P. Perrott,	17 July	1 June 1826	Judgment affirmed on repair hearing.
D°	Dean of Jersey vs. P. Perrott,	17 July		
St. Kitt's	J. F. Barham & another vs. Roger Woodburne,	21 July	18 May 1819	Judgment affirmed on regular hearing.
Berbice	Thomas Wilson by Thomas Fryer Layfield & another vs. William Ross, sq. Hugh Rose,	26 July	9 June 1821	Judgment affirmed on regular hearing.
Jersey	Peter Guichy vs. John Nicolle.	27 July	22 June 1822	Judgment affirmed with costs on regular hearing.
Antigua	William Byam Wyke & others vs. J. R. D. Halliday,	14 August	18 May 1822	Judgment partly reversed and partly affirmed on regular hearing.
St. Vincent's	Gerald Shaw & others vs. Attorney General.	24 August	9 June 1821	Judgment reversed on regular hearing.

Figure 34. Matthew Morry Privy Council Appeal

10 March 1824

CHAPTER EIGHT - CAPLIN BAY AND FERRYLAND

A Brief History of the Fishery in Ferryland and Caplin Bay

I feel a little strange including here a précis of the early history of the fishery in this part of the Southern Shore because it is a subject so second nature to many Newfoundlanders that it is a bit like preaching to the choir. Nevertheless, I have to assume that this book will be read by some non-Newfoundlanders and, in due course, possibly by future generations of readers for whom this will no longer be something they hear about in their youngest years from their elders, as I have done.

Almost everyone in Newfoundland knows already that this area of the Southern Shore was originally settled in 1621 by George Calvert, later Lord Baltimore. The archeological dig of his Colony of Avalon has been producing finds for the museums and the history books for so long now (it began in earnest in 1992, though it was preceded by test digs as early as the 1930s[23]) that an entire generation has been born since its inception and has grown up knowing about this important historical initiative.

But interestingly, we are told that these original settlers were not there to prosecute the rich cod fishery in the area. Apparently, no effort was made by them to do so and all of the activity of these early settlers was land-based, attempting to eke a living out of the thin, infertile soil and inhospitable climate of the area. For that reason alone, amongst several others, the Colony was doomed from the start, and in fact, was abandoned by Calvert and his family in less than a decade. They moved on to New England where they founded what is now the state of Maryland.

Others, however, including a bit of a rogue named David Kirke, who won permission from King Charles I to occupy the plantation – an action challenged by the Calvert family in Court - saw the potential for using the area as a base of operations for the fishery. Apparently, Kirke did not take part in this industry himself but rather served as local Lord and Master (and Publican!) keeping some degree of order in the area and administering to the material needs of those who prosecuted the fishery.

The names of the earliest practitioners of the fishing trade in Ferryland and surrounding areas can be drawn from a number of historical documents such as the list of "Shipps Makinge Fishinge Voyages wt Boatkeepers In Newfoundland -1678"[24] and petitions to the Crown seeking better protection from marauding French and Dutch ships, for there never was an English Garrison in Newfoundland, let alone in Ferryland, for many decades to come.

---

[23] For detailed information on the history of the dig, see http://colonyofavalon.ca/dig/
[24] http://ngb.chebucto.org/Articles/1678-nfld-fishing-masters.shtml

These were the Masters of vessels out of ports in southwest England, notably Bideford and Barnstable in those early days, but almost exclusively Dartmouth in the time of Matthew Morry and his kin and associates. And there were no permanent residents amongst them. They came for the fishing season, from April to December at the latest, set up shore facilities for the processing and drying of the cod, and then returned to England, either directly or via the Iberian Peninsula, mainly Portugal, where the salted fish was traded for wine, consumer goods and salt to start the cycle over again. Each year they vied for the chance to be the first to arrive in each port in Newfoundland, not only as a matter of honour, but more importantly because the first to arrive was declared the "Fishing Admiral" for that port that year. In that capacity, the first to arrive not only was able to claim the choice shore stations for his use, but he also became the law of the land. In Ferryland, however, with a few more or less permanent residents like David Kirke and his wife and sons operating year-round, there must have been some lively debate as to who really was the law of the land.

Before too long, bigger fish (excuse the pun), in the form of well-established business families like the Holdsworths in Ferryland and St. John's and the Newmans and their several associates in Harbour Breton on the south coast and in St. John's, were contending for an increased share of the wealth that the cod afforded. Indeed, after one fateful raid on Ferryland by the French under Pierre Le Moyne d'Iberville and Jacques-François de Brouillan in 1696, which left that settlement entirely in ruins and abandoned, it was Arthur Holdsworth who repopulated the area in the first years of the new century and put Ferryland back on its feet again.

However, during the 18th century, a number of smaller-scale merchants from New England (e.g. Francis Tree, a Loyalist from the Boston Area who acquired a fishing room in Caplin Bay[25], though actually residing in Ferryland) as well as from England (e.g. Robert Carter in Ferryland at least as early as 1842, and Henry J. Sweetland shortly thereafter) set up more or less permanent operations in Ferryland and nearby Caplin Bay, mainly on land that they had not been granted. Grants were almost impossible to obtain until late in the century, due to government policies discouraging settlement as being contrary to the interests of the merchants living in and working from English ports.

Kevin Reddigan, a local historian, born in Calvert, has studied this subject intensively in regard to the early grants in Caplin Bay and had this to say:

> *"They [grants] could be obtained, but initially, they were often only granted to 'people of stature'. However, in the last three decades of the 1700s, restrictions were relaxed. Francis Tree was given his grant in Sept 1773 by the Ferryland Surrogate. One week later, Thomas Nash/Roger McGraugh received their fishery grant, likely after it was forwarded to the Governor for scrutiny, by the Ferryland Surrogate. Matthew Morry's 1784 fishery grant was next, followed by his other grant in 1790... The caveat attached to all of these grants was the same, i.e. that the land could be held in their possession (not owned), as long as it was used for the improvement of the fishery."*

These were certainly amongst the first grants issued on the entire Southern Shore. Strictly speaking, these were not "land

---

[25] I should pause here to explain that Calvert was the name adopted for Caplin Bay in 1922. There were many places known as Caplin Bay around the coast of Newfoundland. In light of the necessities of the postal service being able to consistently and correctly route postal delivery, the Newfoundland Nomenclature Board, in the early 20th century, made efforts to reduce duplication of place names such as these.

grants". Land grants were still virtually unheard of in Newfoundland at the end of the 18th century because the Crown hadn't yet decided that it really wanted to support permanent settlement there. But it was rapidly coming to the conclusion that this was not only inevitable but desirable, for many reasons. And before long, true grants, in perpetuity were being issued without conditions attached, such as the continued use of the premises for the fishery, as was the condition attached to Matthew's first patent.

It should also be noted that, while such grants were given on the strength of representations that the waterside premises that they were seeking to obtain had not been previously occupied by anyone within the living memory of the ancient inhabitants there, other properties that they acquired by purchase were formerly occupied by earlier "planters" who had either died or vacated the area. So, settlement for fishing purposes was certainly taking place prior to 1750.

These latter men, Carter, Sweetland and Tree, amongst a few others, may be considered the forerunners of Matthew Morry as this new breed of relatively smaller-scale merchants who chose to come and reside in Newfoundland rather than operate from England. It took Matthew a very long time to decide to join them. As discussed in the next section, Matthew continued as an itinerant partner for Matthew Morry & Co. for at least three decades and probably longer before finally moving permanently, lock, stock and barrel, to Caplin Bay.

The Seasonal Fishery Years

Let us turn now to the time of Matthew Morry I as an itinerant West Country merchant plying the Newfoundland codfish trade seasonally, whilst keeping a foot in both worlds. This phase of his life and career covered the period between when he first went to sea as a cabin boy or ordinary seaman at age fourteen or so (ca

1764) and when we can say with some certainty that he no longer maintained a residence in Dartmouth (ca 1815), a period of over fifty years.

There is actually no doubt at all that it was never Matthew Morry's intention to remain in Newfoundland. He says as much in one of his Complaints to the High Court of Chancery, intimating that he was in the process of making the final move back to Dartmouth to spend his retirement years when his legal problems with his former partner put a halt to those plans. And the unsuccessful outcome of those court cases and the ruination of his reputation and loss of his property in Dartmouth effectively made the decision to settle in Newfoundland the only option available to him.

That said, and whether or not he would have continued to pay visits to Newfoundland afterwards, he had already planted deep roots in Newfoundland from which his son, Matthew Morry II, had gained the support needed to establish his permanent dynasty in that part of the world (Caplin Bay). This book will finish up in the final chapter with an account of the life of Matthew Morry II, his family and a brief look at some of his most interesting descendants.

It seems most likely that Matthew Morry I's first glimpse of Newfoundland as a young seaman would have been the coast of the Southern Shore, either in Caplin Bay or nearby Ferryland. This was the focus of attention of the large merchant class families with whom he was associated and employed in those days; families like the Holdsworths. Matthew probably got his first taste of life in Newfoundland by having been promoted to Mate on the PORT MERCHANT, which overwintered in Newfoundland in 1772-73, though we are not informed as to which port it remained in that year. But my feeling is that it must have been either Caplin Bay or Ferryland, and it must have been an unusually mild and pleasant winter, because it was to that area that Matthew returned again and again and, when he was well established as a merchant himself, this was where he chose to set up his own fishing rooms. He returned to Dartmouth that spring and married his first wife, Mary Graham, on the 1st of March. But there is no intimation in anything he did from that point forward that he ever intended to move her and his family to Newfoundland.

Figure 35. Caplin Bay early 20th century

Where Matthew Morry had Operated 100 Years Earlier

That said, managing a fishing operation out of Dartmouth without a solid foot on the ground in Newfoundland was simply impossible. As mentioned above, in 1784, with the assistance of Robert Carter, the man who would ultimately become his father-in-law by his second wife, Ann(e) Carter, Matthew successfully petitioned the Governor at the time, Vice-Admiral John Campbell, for a fishing room at the head of Capling [sic] Bay.

Six years later, in 1790, Matthew applied for and received an additional "grant" from Jacob Waller, Captain of HM Ship the

ROSE, who was acting as Surrogate[26] in the area that fall and winter. This grant extended Matthew's holdings in Caplin Bay, subject once again to the pleasure of the then governor, Vice-Admiral Mark Milbanke, and conditional upon his continued occupation and use of the property for the purpose of prosecuting the fishery.

This second parcel was actually referred to in the approval as a "grant" but there was no mention of putting a dwelling house there. However, the location, beside the Gut Pond, and not directly beside the earlier plot, suggests that it was here that Matthew Morry may have built his original dwelling. We must assume that prior to that time he would have rented premises for his seasonal sojourns in Newfoundland, since there is no evidence of his having ever built a home there previously, not having a right of any kind to any land on which to do so. He did build what was called a "shoreman's house" on his original grant. Perhaps he used that himself for some years.

Here, once again, I must defer to Kevin Reddigan's more in-depth knowledge of the settlement of Caplin Bay:

> "Unfortunately, there are no details of early dwellings at Caplin Bay. I know that an "old house" belonging to the Holdsworths existed at The Beach prior to 1786. That 'old house' was demolished in the winter of 1785, due to a blunder by Thomas Gibbs, Matthew Morry's fishery partner... Matthew Morry eventually built his shoreman's house in 1786, on his own 1784 granted land. There are no references as to where Matthew laid his head while at Caplin Bay, possibly

---

[26] Surrogate was a loose term applied to individuals with no training in law who were appointed to act as judges of a sort in the absence of trained legal specialists. Initially surrogates were mainly naval officers but later were civilians.

aboard his ship, or in some other temporary summer shelter. The shoreman's house (the bunkhouse) could have been used, but its main purpose was to house the Company's many migrant fishermen/servants/dieters, etc. Probably a very noisy and raucous place. We can speculate that there was some substantial dwelling built by the time that Matthew Morry II settled on the South Side, but no hints of the overall living accommodations for Matthew I, Matthew II, and John Morry have been uncovered... from a resident settlement point of view, it was pretty low key, but I would suggest that the area, in and around, the Morry fishing area, was very much a beehive of activity especially during the fishing season."

The census taken of communities in the Ferryland District by Robert Carter in 1800 showed that there were only five families actually living in Caplin Bay[27]. By contrast, or comparison, Peter E. Pope, in his book "Fish into Wine – The Newfoundland Plantation in the Seventeenth Century", reports that:

"When officers of the Royal Navy took the first censuses of English Newfoundland in the 1670s, Ferryland itself consisted of about a dozen planter households, and adjacent Caplin Bay generally had one or two plantations."

Not much sign of growth in 130 years. He mentions John Slaughter as one planter present at least a couple of decades earlier

---

[27] It is important to note that, according to Robert Cuff in "Newfoundland and Labrador – Insiders Perspective", in 1785 there were only 10,000 people in all of Newfoundland, and this number would not have increased much before the mass migrations from England and Ireland that accompanied the boom in the fishery during the War of 1812, when opportunities in the fishery, then a monopoly for Newfoundlanders, were numerous and promising.

and Christopher Pollard was there in 1679, but neither family has descendants present today, Slaughter's Pond being the only recollection of these earliest settlers.

The Morrys were not listed amongst the five families in Caplin Bay in 1800. Nor were the Sweetlands, with whom the Morrys were so intimately entwined later. Evidence suggests that, like Matthew, the Sweetland's obtained through some means (some purchased, some leased from the Holdsworth family) several areas of the southside to use for their fishing enterprises starting in about 1814. In the 1800 Census mentioned above, only Anne, then a widow, and Benjamin Sweetland, her youngest son, were listed, in Ferryland, not Caplin Bay, suggesting that her older sons, Henry and William, were then away being educated in England, as was normal for the children of English merchant families at the time. Henry Sweetland Sr. died in Ferryland in 1791 and the Sweetland operations in Caplin Bay were started by his sons.

Although Matthew's first wife, Mary Graham, had died four years before, clearly, he had not taken the huge step yet to relocate with the younger members of his family as early as this. In fact, only the two youngest, Matthew and Esther, probably ever came to Newfoundland, and the latter returned and lived her life as a spinster in Dartmouth.

Kevin Reddigan has made it his life's work to gather the scattered pieces of information that exist and draw up as complete a picture as possible of the settlement of Caplin Bay. On his website, Family Names of Calvert (Caplin Bay), Newfoundland (http://calvertweb.ca/) it is possible to find just about every bit of information available on this topic, together with Kevin's educated guesses, which are necessary to fill in the many gaps. From this study, it is possible to say that there was limited settlement at Caplin Bay as early as 1663. But permanent settlement followed much later, likely in the early eighteenth century. Here are Kevin's thoughts on where that took place:

"I think it is safe to say that the earliest permanent settlement of Caplin Bay likely occurred at the head of the bay. Here the bay ended in a large wide beach, which in addition to providing a natural surface for drying salted codfish, served as a breakwater with an access to a salt-water pond. This pond was accessible from Caplin Bay through a narrow channel known as "The Gut", which was wide and deep enough to allow small boats access to safe anchorage within the sheltered Gut Pond (also called Caplin Bay Pond in some earlier documents). At the head of this pond, a waterfall provided an abundance of fresh drinking water. Caplin Bay also had a variety of trees, growing down to the water's edge. This resource was suitable for firewood and provided building material for fishing premises, houses, and other forms of shelter."

Clearly, Kevin is describing the areas where Matthew Morry's two grants were located. But equally clearly, those areas had been settled, or at least employed in the fishery, long before Matthew took possession of the granted lands. Yet in both cases, testimony was offered that the choice areas in question had never been occupied for a very long time, forty years or more. This is somewhat of a mystery, for why would Matthew have been able to make such a contention and win the support of the governors at the time if this was not the case? Kevin indicates that somehow the Holdsworth family had claim to land and waterside premises in this area as well as in Ferryland (the latter purchased by John Henry Morry in 1844) and that this property in Caplin Bay somehow changed hands and became the so-called "Nash Plantation" that was leased by, and then purchased by, the Morry family in 1855. But none of this explains why no one else was occupying the choice lands where Matthew Morry's grants were given, nor where he was able to find a habitation to rent and in which to live before he built his own house. And indeed, we have no idea where the house he eventually built or bought was located. Later voters' lists show various members of the Morry family living in virtually every area of Caplin Bay from the south side, to the head of the Bay, to the north side, where the area known as Athlone became the last Morry property in Caplin Bay (by then renamed Calvert), with the death of Miss Lizzie Morry in 1930.

This was the same Elizabeth Morry mentioned above in regard to the loss of the Morry business papers and the eleven volumes of the Complete Works of William Shakespeare that had originally belonged to Matthew Morry I and then transferred to son and grandson of the same name, the latter being Miss Lizzie's father. As for Matthew Morry I himself, nothing is known with certainty of the location of his actual abode in these early days.

The Sweetlands first and only abode in Caplin Bay (they had formerly lived in Ferryland) is far better known. In fact, Gerald L. Pocius, in his book "A Place to Belong – Community Order and Everyday Space in Calvert, Newfoundland", provides a photo of how it still appeared in the early twentieth century after it was first renovated and another of a much smaller house built on its foundation to accommodate the simpler needs of the modern residents. The size of these houses gives some sense of the wealth of those engaged in the cod fishery out of Caplin Bay in those days.

Figure 36. Athlone and its Last Occupant Miss Lizzie Morry

ca 1930

Figure 37. Sweetland House, Then and Now

Matthew Morry and his Second Wife, Anne Carter

Strange to say, it isn't really known when exactly Matthew Morry remarried. We know it was before the court cases in which he was embroiled with his former partner, Walter Prideaux, because the latter minced no words in denigrating Anne and her sons by her previous marriage to Henry Sweetland, claiming that she was taking advantage of her marriage to Matthew Morry to live lavishly off the assets of Matthew Morry & Co. and even to draw business away from that company to divert to Sweetland & Co. We also know that he was still a migratory fish merchant at the time that Anne's father took his 1800 census of the Ferryland area. But there is no evidence of a church record of their marriage, either at the district Anglican registry in Petty Harbour or at the Anglican Cathedral in St. John's. I now suspect that they may not have married until after 1813, because an agreement between Matthew Sr. and Jr. (a sort of power of attorney or living will in case Matthew Senior never made it back from one of his many forays to attend Court in England) signed in that year indicated that the elder Matthew was still a resident of Dartmouth at the time. Therefore, their marriage must have been very recent indeed, probably just before Prideaux took exception to it.

If I am correct and they married in about 1814, this would make them both seventy-four at the time. Obviously, as stated before, this was a marriage of convenience for both of them. It provided entrée for Matthew into a closed society. It provided Anne with a third merchant marine husband, having profited from her marriages to two men of similar stature previously. And it also allowed for collaboration rather than competition between Matthew Morry & Co. and Sweetland & Co. A community as small as Caplin Bay could not sustain two such independent entities.

The Morrys of Caplin Bay and Their Kin

By the time Matthew Morry, and later his sons and grandsons, began to participate in the seasonal fish trade in the late 1700s and then take up residence in Caplin Bay and Ferryland in the early 1800s, they were undoubtedly looked upon by the well-established traders in the community as "Johnny-come-latelies" or, as we shall see, even looked down upon as carpetbaggers and social inferiors by some in the merchant class. They quickly went about establishing themselves in society by forming partnerships, both in business and through marriage, with all the established merchant-class families from Aquaforte to Cape Broyle.

Finding one's place in society when moving into a new community is never easy. It probably took at least a generation for the Morrys to be fully accepted as equals by the established merchant class elite. They seem to have enjoyed acceptance after that, though how they were looked upon by the workers they employed is another matter!

But resentment persisted, at least among some of their peers. Two poems, written by an Anne Carter (most likely Anne Catherine Weston Carter), *The Motley Maggot Gang* and *The Grinder*, bear uncomplimentary references to the Morrys and, in the case of the latter, to some of the other contemporary merchant class families in the area.

A Song – The Motley Maggot Gang
Anne Carter (most probably Anne Catherine Weston Carter)
ca 1850

A Song

A set of rogues are in this town
Who truth and justice both disown
They are a petty pygmy clan
And named the motley maggot gang

> Chorus
> Sing loud the motley maggot gang
> Sing ho the motley maggot gang
> Come join my chorus every one
> And echo loud the maggot gun

The poor they oft oppress and wrong
And cloak it mong their giling throng
They are a bandit wicked clan
And named the motley maggot gang

> Sing loud the motley etc. etc.

James Costly was nigh rob'd tis clear
By lob the dog & sterile steer
A mob they raised his case to bang
Now named the motley maggot gang

> Sing loud etc. etc.

Gainst sheriff tree those rogues conspire
With wicked hate and savage ire
He was too lenient to the clan
The cozening motley maggot gang.

> Sing loud etc. etc.

Poor orphan cannons they took in
Oh what a cruel crying sin

The cozening robers ought to hang
The tyrant motley maggot gang

There's mathew, john, bill, tom and all
With greedy hate they would make fall
They're cruel neros every one
Who form the motley maggot gang.

        Sing loud etc. etc.

I struggled for the longest time trying to figure out which Anne Carter this was and when it was written. It is found amongst the Carter Papers (MG 31) at The Rooms and there is nothing in that file to identify the author or the year it was written. It was only by recognizing the names of the people mentioned and the approximate date that the events presented took place that I could be absolutely sure that this was not written by Matthew Morry I's wife, Anne Carter, as a private rant about her husband's family. The people and events were of the next generation, that is to say, the "Motley Maggot Gang" was the family of Matthew Morry II! With the assistance of my old reliable research partners, Kevin Reddigan and Enid O'Brien, I was able to piece together the events mentioned.

Anne Catherine Weston Carter is most likely the sole author of a number of harsh satirical poems/songs concerning the members of the merchant class in Ferryland whom she looked down upon, including the Morrys. *The Motley Maggot Gang* is one; *The Grinder* is another.

It seems clear that the "Motley Maggot Gang" to which she refers was the Morrys (the Christian names given in the last stanza are those of that generation of Morrys), though I have no idea why she judged them so harshly and apparently bore them so much ill will. In so far as Anne was concerned at least, the Morry family ill-treated James "Costly" (Costello) and one of the "Cannon"

(Canning) family. Alfred of that family was taken in when he was orphaned by the widow of Matthew III, Elizabeth Coulman, but considering when the poem was written, there must have been an earlier Canning, possibly the father or mother of Alfred, whom the author felt the Morrys had mistreated. Kevin thought that maybe Anne believed that the Morrys taking in Canning orphans was not altruistic but rather a means to get free labour. They also apparently were thought to have conspired against Sheriff Philip Tree (or his brother Francis, both of whom were sheriffs), even though she believed that they had been given light treatment by him for whatever crimes they are thought by her to have committed. These allusions are all clear, but the cause of her ire is not.

Willeen Keough, in her published Ph. D. treatise "The Slender Thread - Irish Women on the Southern Avalon, 1750-1869" mentions this song/poem and explains that the reference to James Costello would have had to do with an animal maiming, a common form of protest against the landowners by the Irish which was imported to Newfoundland.

Kevin Reddigan added the following commentary:

"While Alfred Canning regarded himself as an adopted son, the contrary view was held within the Morry clan. This view is expressed in one letter that was written by a niece of Mrs. Eliza Morry [wife of Matthew Morry III, the woman who took in Alfred] which read:
Aunt Eliza was a foolish woman. When she took Alf Canning, she did not adopt him or give him her name. He was left without a mother and none of the neighbours wanted him."

The second poem is called *The Grinder* (ca 1850 From PANL MG 31 - The Carter Papers) This is another of the poems/songs written by Anne Carter criticising the members of the merchant class that she found to not meet her high moral expectations. In the poem/song called *The Motley Maggot Gang,* she took aim primarily at the Morrys. Here the scope of her ire seems to have broadened to include another late-coming merchant family, the Stabbs. Underlying this tirade there appears to be an implication that someone took advantage of her and then wrote about it or otherwise spread rumours defaming her reputation. The mention of "Northside" where the Morrys were the principal, if not the only, merchant class family then in residence, and the allusion to "Harry" and his "scandal-proof homespun connections" seems to implicate John Henry Morry (my 2nd Great Grandfather). He was known as Harry and was likely the only Morry resident there at the time. He had also married a Winsor/Windsor - one of the old merchant class families - giving him scandal-proofing to some extent. Two of his brothers married Carter women, which may explain the phrase "they say we are sons of one mother" since he now shared a kinship with Anne.

Enid O'Brien also elaborated on the obvious allusion to the Stabb family and amplified:

"I was wondering if she was speaking about the Stabbs? As you know, Ewen Stabb was married to Ann Carter Tessier, daughter of Joan Carter/Peter Tessier and they had fishing rooms in Ferryland as early as 1823 (Ref Encyclopedia of NL). I was wondering if the "itinerant quack" might refer to Ewen's brother, Dr. Henry H Stabb. Ewen came out in support of Henry John Boulton, who was supposed to be a very "bad" judge, and I thought the reference to "vicar and moses" might refer to the clergy being asleep while the judge did what he wanted."

The allegorical and satirical figure of Vicar and Moses was popular at the time, as it had been produced in Staffordshire pottery and was a commonly available household ornament. It referred back to Hogarth's engraving of a vicar asleep in his pulpit while his clerk "Moses" delivered his sermon to a sleeping congregation. In other words, Anne was saying that the people of Ferryland were asleep at the switch while all of these wrongdoings were going on around them. The reference to "ballanamoni" is curious. Ballinamona House is in County Waterford, Ireland, and there is a crossroads in Tipperary North Riding known as Ballinamona Cross. This seems to refer to someone from one of those two areas, but who that could be is a mystery at this time. The first person to come under her attack is identified only by his initials "L. B.". At the moment this person remains anonymous. Suffice it to say, there were very few members of the merchant class that came up to the high standards of Anne Carter!

The Grinder

1. *In this isle many places we'll find where there's love, friendship, union and concord but ferryland what shame and disgrace we see nothing but disunion and discord attackting [sic] defenceless females unmanly and beasts we do find them in union let honest men join and the venomous scribblers we'll grind'em*

(chorus) L.B. first as many supposes some folks at the northside come next sir the author of vicar and moses and ballanamoni nix sir

2. *The manie do not stop here some folks imitating their betters stabb private characters we here though not knowing much about letters then note-taking harry beware drop your scandal-proof homespun connections to lash you i mean to forbear its meerly for want of reflection chorus) come neighbours join in the cause the scribbling trash - we will bind them who act against morals and laws O damn their eyes we will grind'(em)*

3. *Few words to the intinerent quack who absconded some years since for scandal if dissention he means to beat a reformer of messina we'll handle let folks*

*their own business mind in harmony join one-
another by allusions they see I'm not blind they say
we are sons of one mother chorus) come neighbours
join in the cause &*

4. *Men and women in this place its no lie who daily
traduce each other not seeing the beam in their eye
but enlarging the mote in another hypocritical
canting elves no honour they have none are blinder
the first I find out in protest I'll give them a task of
my grinder*

*NB. done in the harbour of Ferryland by a philanthrophist
[sic] who holds in detestation the infamous proceedings of
people - some of good abilities but yet to men of sense most
appear silly who delight like assassins in the dark
contemplating their dire deeds with delight! shame! oh!*

shame to the thing called man! for man he cannot be called who wantonly attacks defenceless women and exults behind the scenes, at the thought of his infamous lying [missing word] ...tions! [28]

It has been widely debated amongst Morry family historians when, if ever, Matthew and Anne moved from Caplin Bay to Ferryland. Matthew had no holdings in the latter, whereas Anne did, from at least one of her former husbands and from her father. She also held property, along with her two sons who were engaged in the fishery, in Caplin Bay. So, there may have been no incentive for either of them to shift to Ferryland, other than that it was a larger village and considered almost like the capital of the Southern Shore.

We know from voting lists assembled in the mid-1800s that the Morrys (sons and grandsons of Matthew) were still occupying residences in various parts of Caplin Bay. Matthew Morry II shows up each year in the Voters Lists for Caplin Bay 1840 - 1859 (for every year until his death in 1856) variously listed as Esq., Sr. and JP, to distinguish between him and his son, who also appears in all these years from 1844-1852. The senior Matthew has "Rocky Park" shown as his specific domicile area on all voters lists but one, and it is not only possible but likely that he never moved during this period because the designations alternate back and forth from year to year and may have represented the same

---

[28] Unfortunately, the bottom of the page is frayed and one line is partially missing

location. No Morry shows up in the Voters List for Ferryland 1840-1859 until John Henry's name (my second great grandfather, the grandson of Matthew I) appears in 1849 with "North Side" given as his specific domicile. In 1855 and 1859 he is joined on the list by his brothers Henry (South Side) and Arthur (North Side) in that order, who evidently moved from Caplin Bay at that time (their names appeared on the list for Caplin Bay before that). But it can be accepted that John Henry moved to Ferryland in 1844, when he and his partner/brother-in-law Peter Paint Le Messurier bought the Holdsworth premises, including the massive old stone house, from Arthur William Olive Holdsworth, great-grandson of the Arthur Holdsworth who apparently had the house built for him when the family was still actively involved in the Newfoundland fishery in the mid-1700s.

So, on balance, I feel comfortable in stating that the Morry family remained in Caplin Bay from the day Matthew moved there permanently, after his trials (literally) and tribulations in England around 1819. I doubt very much that he stayed in Dartmouth long enough to be witness to the humiliation of being held responsible, in part, for the unlawful withdrawal of the funds from his grandson's inheritance.

Regardless of where they were operating from at the time, the two family-owned and operated companies of the Sweetlands and the Morrys essentially functioned as one from the day of Matthew's marriage to Anne. In that regard, Walter Prideaux was probably correct. The Maritime History Archive's CD database entitled "Ships and Seafarers of Atlantic Canada" sheds light on who owned and who manned vessels operating in the Newfoundland fishery from 1787 to 1936. And the vessels associated with the Morrys during this time were co-owned by the Sweetlands:

- The IRIS was initially co-owned in thirds by William and Benjamin Sweetland and Matthew Morry J$^{r.}$ (II) from

1820 to 1825 but sole ownership was transferred to Henry Sweetland in 1826
- The ECLIPSE was originally co-owned by William and Benjamin Sweetland between 1820 and 1825 but then William transferred his share to Matthew Morry in 1825
- The SNIPE FISH was originally co-owned by Benjamin Sweetland and Matthew Morry in 1829 to 1831 and registration was then renewed until 1842 with the same two owners.

There were two exceptions on record to the Morry-Sweetland co-ownership of vessels:

- The MIRIAM was owned outright by John Morry between 1839 and 1840. This was my great grandfather, John Henry Morry, the son of Matthew Morry II.
- The JESSIE was owned outright by William Sweetland, Henry's son, when he moved to Bonavista; it was an old vessel originally built and registered in Bonavista Bay in 1887 and still operating in 1932.

The IRIS was lost at sea whilst solely owned by Lieut. Henry Sweetland (RN), son of Anne Carter and Capt. Henry J. Sweetland. Lieut. Sweetland took a break from his service in the RN to work as Mate on the DORSETSHIRE, owned by Matthew Morry and Co., and was on her when she was captured as a prize by a French privateer in 1804 but then retaken by his colleagues in the Royal Navy. This was the event in which Matthew Morry's cousin, Richard Morrey, was Master and was taken back to France with all of the rest of the crew except Sweetland, who was retained to help operate the vessel. As mentioned above, Richard Morrey died in a French prison the following year.

During the period that these vessels were in operation, the fishery in Newfoundland took a tumble. Kevin Major notes that:

"In 1825, the people of the outports found themselves victims once again of the fluctuating markets for cod. The price paid for their fish had taken a sudden plunge."

It seems likely that this had a devastating effect on the bottom line of the Morry and Sweetland enterprises. Not long after that William and Benjamin Sweetland both applied for and won positions as Magistrates in Bonavista and Trinity, respectively, and William, in fact, was working as an agent for William Vallance, a Water St. Merchant, as early as 1826. His brother, Benjamin, was still listed as a merchant from Ferryland at the time that he married Tryphena Gaden, the daughter of a wealthy St. John's merchant, in 1827, but it is likely this marriage had economic motivations for him. In any event, the Sweetland reign in Caplin Bay was essentially over by 1830 and their premises were put on the auction block. Parts of it were still up for grabs years later when my second great granduncle, Thomas Graham Morry, was acting on their behalf to try and dispose of it.

Figure 38. Silhouette of Lieut. Henry Sweetland, RN

CHAPTER NINE – FIRST GENERATION NEWFOUNDLANDERS

Matthew Morry II's Family

We are close now to the end of this story about one of the last West Country Merchants who came and stayed in Newfoundland. Matthew Morry I lived to the ripe old age of 86 and was buried in 1836, along with his grandson, John Foale Morry, as mentioned above, in the old Anglican Cemetery in Ferryland (often known as the Forge Hill or Fox Hill Cemetery) associated with the now-vanished St. Luke's Church.

Figure 39. Gravestone of Matthew Morry and Grandson

His second wife, Anne Carter, who had already outlived two husbands, also outlived Matthew by two years. We know her date of burial (15 September 1838) but can only speculate as to the place where she is buried since very few of the gravestones in the two old cemeteries in Ferryland are still visible above ground and legible.

But before we say farewell to Matthew Morry I, it will be interesting to see how his son of the same name made out after planting himself and his family in the new land, since his was the first family of Morrys entirely born and brought up in Newfoundland.

The family group sheet for the extensive family of Matthew Morry II and his wife, Anne Saunders is found in Appendix 2.

The first thing one cannot help but notice in this report is the size of the family. For an Irish Catholic family of that day, this would not be a remarkably large family, but it would have been for an English Protestant merchant-class family.

Another notable fact, compared to the family group sheets of the earlier generations of the family in Devon, is that the specific details for each person are more complete. Perhaps this only stands to reason because of the fact that this family existed in relatively "modern" times where one might expect to have better records. But, in truth, the church records for Caplin Bay in those days were certainly no better than those in Dartmouth or Stoke Gabriel a century or two before. Rather, the records kept by the family had improved markedly in this generation, partially because of the general level of literacy in the family, and partly because of it being the first generation of children in a merchant class family.

This latter distinction also is demonstrated by the fact that this is the first generation of the family in which individual portraits of family members exist, whether as paintings, daguerreotypes or early, primitive photographs. Here are four of them[29]:

---

[29] Refer back to the caption on the cover photo of this book. While I do not personally ascribe to the belief prevalent in the family that the oil painting portrait shown here is that of Matthew Morry III (I believe it is a portrait of his grandfather, Matthew Morry I), I am outnumbered in this regard and must acknowledge this majority opinion.

Figure 40. Portraits of Four Sons of Matthew II

Matthew III[30], John Henry, Frederick Clift and Robert Morry ca 1850

---

[30] See note above on Title page pertaining to this book's cover photo

Matthew Morry II effectively ran the Morry enterprises in Caplin Bay during the time, and probably long before, his father was fighting his Court battles in England, and it seems from the records that his father never played an active role in the company after that time. Which is understandable since he was in his seventies by then.

Along with his stepbrothers and sometime-partners, the Sweetlands, Matthew Morry II effectively controlled the fishing activity out of Caplin Bay for years to come. But by the time his sons were old enough to become actively involved, competition existed from a hitherto unknown quarter; the Irish bye-boat keepers were now becoming merchants in their own rights and several of them in both Caplin Bay and Ferryland were beginning to dominate the local economy.

I won't go into the life and times of each of the children of this family except to indicate how their careers and lifestyles were directly associated with the family enterprise.

Thomas Graham Morry

This Thomas could be referred to as Thomas Graham Morry II because, as we have seen above, he was named for a son of Matthew Morry I who died almost certainly whilst leading the life of a Privateer along with his brother John. The name Thomas Graham Morry has carried down in every generation including my older brother.

Thomas began his career as the agent for Newman and Company in St. John's and was, in fact, responsible for the design and construction of the Newman vaults and Newman House, in which he lived while employed by the company. He later moved on to a career in marine insurance. He is thought to be the first of the Morrys to depart the Southern Shore for greener pastures. Not surprising really considering the number of sons in the family, far exceeding the number that could make a comfortable living as fish merchants without treading on each others' toes.

Figure 41. Newman House, 1 Springdale Street, St. John's

Matthew Morry III

The second son, Matthew Morry III continued the family enterprise, branching out and attempting to take advantage of the Labrador migrant fishery and the seal hunt. He was said to be a bit of a "hard ticket" in his youth, fond of the bottle, as were many of the Morry men, and quite a ladies man (ditto). But he made up for this by showing his humanity and taking for his first wife, Elizabeth Chafe of Petty Harbour, who was then dying of consumption and who said she would die happy if Matthew would marry her. He did, and they were married on July 18, 1838. Four days later she was buried in her wedding dress. His magnanimity in this gesture was not forgotten and a generation later a boy in the family was christened in his honour, Matthew Morey Chafe.

Capt. William Sweetland Morry

A younger brother, William Sweetland Morry was a well-known sea captain who sailed the world's oceans encountering many adventures that would make a book in themselves. For instance, he was once almost lynched in Boston for standing up for the Queen. Whether because of that or not, it was also recorded that he once circumnavigated the globe without once setting foot in any of the foreign ports he visited.

In Morry's Cove, beneath Athlone, there is a tall stone named Long Will in his honour. It is said that he used to moor his sailing vessels to this stone when in his home port. William died on dry land, but his son of the same name (William Sweetland Morry), who was also a sea captain, died at the age of twenty-one when a decrepit ship he was hired to captain and take to Wales with a load of coal sank with the loss of all hands on board. It was said that he foresaw this fate once he took charge of the vessel beside the wharf in St. John's and paid off the crewmen he had hired from Caplin Bay and sent them home, thus saving their lives. His fate was shared by far too many in the Morry family tree. His young widow, Clara Isabelle Windsor, who later became the second wife of my great grandfather, Thomas Graham Morry, made this memorial to William, which is found in St. Philip's Anglican Church in Aquaforte:

Figure 42. Memorial to William Sweetland Morry, Aquaforte

Mary Morry and Peter Paint Le Messurier

The first daughter in the family, Mary, married Peter Paint Le Messurier, of St. Peter's Port, Guernsey, coming from a fish merchant family on that island. Peter became the partner of her brother (my second great grandfather), John Henry Morry, in the purchase of the Holdsworth properties in Ferryland. When that enterprise proved not as successful as they had hoped, Peter was also forced to move to St. John's, due to increased competition for a diminishing resource, and there became a clerk and then a businessman in his own right. One of their sons was named Matthew Morry Le Messurier.

Figure 43. Mary Morry Le Messurier ca 1850

John Henry Morry

My second great grandfather, John Henry Morry, was the next child of the family in chronological order. As just mentioned, in 1844 he acquired the Holdsworth holdings in Ferryland and thus became the first Morry to move from Caplin Bay to Ferryland.

However, he too was one of those men whose reach exceeded his grasp, and it was not possible for him and Peter Paint Le Messurier to make the final payment to Arthur William Olive Holdsworth. They were bailed out by John's mother-in-law, Anne Coulman Winsor, who had money from inheritance from the Coulman family as well as a well-to-do husband, Capt. Peter Winsor, who died in 1850.

As a side-note, it was Ann Coulman Winsor's bible that was noted earlier as an object lesson to new genealogists not to take as proven the vital statistics found in family bibles. Virtually none of the entries in her bible have proven accurate.

John pursued the fish business, specialising in by-products like cod liver oil to try and skirt around the increasing competition. But his business was not very successful and he eventually moved to St. John's in his later years and operated a boarding house called the Morry House at 159 Gower St. Before departing Ferryland, however, he continued to occupy the old stone Holdsworth House and raised his family there, even though it was, in effect the property of his mother-in-law, along with all of his lands and waterside premises.

Figure 44. Ann Coulman Winsor ca 1890

Figure 45. Howard Morry beside the Holdsworth Stone[31]

He never was able to repay her loan from the proceeds of his business. Late in her life, Ann transferred ownership of these properties for a nominal $1 and the "natural affection" of a grandmother to her grandson, Thomas Graham Morry III, my great grandfather. However, she stipulated that the house should remain available to his two maiden sisters as long as they remained single. They never married and they outlived him, but neither ever lived in the house or even rented it out. It is said that they did so to spite him because he had married a Roman Catholic.

---

[31] There is a caption on the reverse of this photo written by Dad Morry. It reads in part: "Our boundary stone of the property we bought from Sir Arthur Holdsworth in 1824." In actual fact, Arthur Holdsworth was not knighted, and the property was not purchased until 1844 by Dad Morry's grandfather, John Henry Morry. The "H" on the stone designated "Holdsworth" and the stone itself was reputed to have been brought over from Devon as it was not of a kind found locally. Sadly, the stone was either taken or destroyed in my lifetime and no longer exists.

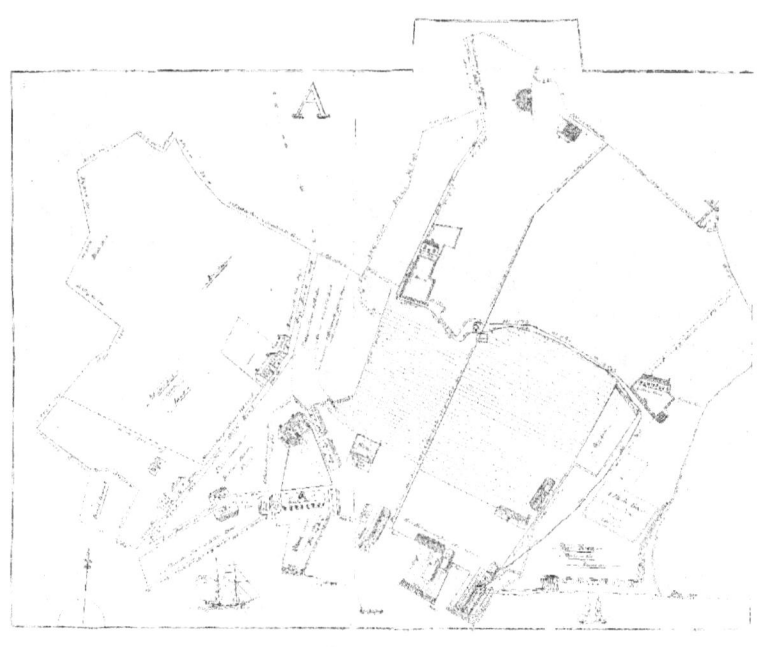

Figure 46. Ferryland Northside Holdsworth Premises ca 1840

Figure 47. John Henry Morry, his Daughters and Niece

Standing on the doorstep of the Holdsworth House ca 1890

An interesting side-note to this mixed marriage. As was obligatory in such cases, the Catholic Church insisted that the groom sign a "sub conditione" agreement to have all children baptised and raised in the faith, and he was true to his word, though he was a staunch C of E man himself. However, without his knowledge, his maiden sisters stole away each child shortly after it was born to have it christened at St. Luke's Anglican church.

In the end, Thomas never did get to occupy the Holdsworth House as an adult, though he was born in the house. Eventually, the passage of years and the challenging climate in Ferryland took their toll and my grandfather had to tear down the old stone house after his return from WWI and built his own, much more modest, home on the foundations.

Benjamin Sweetland Morry

Benjamin Sweetland Morry (another son given the middle name of the closely connected Sweetland family) was also involved in the cod liver oil business but like his brother, John Henry, was not able to make a stable living from that alone and also served as a clerk and storekeeper for the Carter family, the long-established and dominant merchants in Ferryland. Like many of the Morrys, he was successful in being granted a sinecure as a member of the Board of Road Commissioners. All of these sidelines showed how diminished the cod fishery had become over the middle years of the 19th century and also demonstrated how impossible it became for all the sons of any merchant family to remain effectively employed in the fishing and shipping trades in a small outport community such as Ferryland. He too wound up eventually moving to St. John's and operating a boarding house there.

Henry Sweetland Morry

Maintaining the tradition of adding Sweetland to their names, the next child of Matthew Morry II and his wife was Henry Sweetland Morry. Henry managed to make a living in the fish business and died a relatively old man at the home of his daughter,

Esther Graham Morry (III) Carew, who had married Capt. Henry Carew (reputedly a well-known smuggler) in Shores Cove, Cape Broyle. It is said that Henry Carew had his boat painted two different colours on the two sides so that when he sailed out of port en route to St. Pierre the Customs Officer would see one boat leaving and when he returned with a load of contraband the Customs Officer would see a different boat and not put two and two together! A dubious tale, unless the Customs Officers of the day were a lot simpler than they are today.

Henry Sweetland Morry, it turns out, is the ancestor of most of the American Morrys who started out in Newfoundland. His son, George William Morry, headed out to the Klondike to make his fortune, arrived too late to stake a claim, went on to Alaska and struck it rich, and then settled in Seattle, Washington to live off his fortune. Another of Henry's sons, John, was a successful businessman in Fermeuse and St. John's and he and his wife died leaving a fortune to various charities and churches in town. Henry also had a son named after him who was a constable in the Royal Newfoundland Constabulary, the first of a number of Morrys to be associated with the force, including my late uncle Bill.

Capt. Arthur Kemp Morry

The next son was Capt. Arthur Kemp Morry, a sea captain like so many other Morrys, who later settled on land and became a businessman in Old Perlican. It is said he was such a disreputable man in his youth that the parents of the woman he wanted to marry, Mary Oxenham Carter, of the same Carter family as the unidentified Anne Carter who showed such disdain for the Morrys in her poems, would not hear of Mary marrying him. So, he got a group of friends to assist him putting a ladder up to her window and manhandled several large chests of her things, as well as the would-be bride, and took her off in his vessel to be married. It was said by my grandfather that it was an unhappy marriage for her because he never gave up his fondness for the bottle. In consequence, she was buried in Caplin Cove, Conception Bay, whilst he is buried in the old Anglican graveyard in Ferryland.

Priscilla Anne Morry

The next child born was the first of three in the family to be named Priscilla Anne Morry, the first two dying in infancy. That name is said to hold a special curse in the Morry family. No one given the name has ever lived to adulthood or, if they did, died young. One wonders why people persisted in naming their daughters thusly. But they did, and there have been many Morry children named Priscilla, including one of my aunts, who also died in childhood. Dad Morry tells the tale that one of the Priscillas (he calls her his aunt, but he did not have an actual aunt of that name, so it must be a term he used without regard to the generation) was in the fields near the old house in Ferryland and commented to her sister about the odd funeral procession heading up to the church on the main road. What was unusual was that all the mourners, led by her uncle Henry, were walking in front of the hearse instead of behind, as usual. Her sister looked to where Priscilla was pointing and saw nothing. A week later, Priscilla died of diphtheria (a contagion responsible for more deaths in the Morry family than drowning), and sure enough, because of the direction the wind was blowing from, the mourners were told to walk in front of the hearse in order not to come into contact with the germs. Take this for what it's worth!

Frederick Clift Morry

Next, we have another colourful fellow, Frederick Clift Morry. If you have a closer look at his photo in the group of four photos above, the object in his hands is called a "pepperpot", and it was an early version of a six-shot revolver that came out very briefly in the early 1850s before being replaced by the Colt and other true revolvers. I own this daguerreotype but sadly not the pepperpot. There is a story behind how the daguerreotype came into existence and how it wound up coming down through the family to me. Fred was another of the adventuresome ones in the family and he headed off to take part in the Australian gold rush, in the mid-1850s. It is said that he was successful in making a small fortune and that he converted his earnings into a sheep station and water marketing business (the latter of which at least is a matter of historical record) near Geelong, in what is now the state of Victoria but was then New South Wales. At some point, he evidently decided he had enough of living so far from home and sold his share of the business to his partner. He boarded ship for home but never made it. He went overboard in the Indian Ocean somewhere and there are conflicting tales of how that occurred. Dad Morry told the tale this way in a letter to Aunt Jean (keep in mind he was a consummate storyteller and never let the facts get in the way of a good yarn!):

"Your Uncle Fred left school in England and went to Australia to the gold fields when he was eighteen. He got some gold and

invested in sheep. Had a big sheep ranch. He was coming home for a visit. Lizzie had a letter from him and his will. He left all to her as she was his favorite niece. She never got the ranch and only 1500 pounds of his money. It was a six months voyage to Australia at that time and t'was impossible to get to do anything about the will. Well he got sun stroke on the way home. He was going to the gold rush in California in 1849. He jumped into the Indian Ocean crazy with sun stroke. He had a long black cloak lined with Red silk or satin and a big silver clasp in the neck of it. When the boat rowed up and the man grabbed it, He [Frederick] just reached up and undid the buckle and sank. Lizzie had the cape. So, Jean, your ancestors were wild men. Guess the Scotch blood."

The cloak, with this daguerreotype in the pocket, was indeed returned to his closest living relative in Caplin Bay, Miss Lizzie Morry, whom we have discussed before. The daguerreotype made it into the hands of Dad Morry and from him to Aunt Jean and from her, after her death, to me, thanks to the characteristic generosity of her daughter, Karen Chapman. I was able to have it professionally restored by a specialist, Mike Robinson, and his students at Ryerson University free of charge in exchange for giving his students a project to work on. Unfortunately, the salt water damage was too severe to completely correct.

There is another denouement to this story that says a lot about the superstitious nature of people in small outport communities, just as does the curse of the name Priscilla. The story of Fred's misadventure on the way home got around in Caplin Bay and was altered in being told and retold so that it came out to be that the poor man was thrown overboard in the Indian Ocean by robbers taking his gold and that months later his great cloak washed up on the beach in Morry's Cove where Miss Lizzie found it!

The next two children died as infants, George and the second Priscilla Anne.

Robert Morry

The next child to survive to adulthood was Robert (whose photograph appears above). Like several of his brothers, Robert started out as a mariner, earning his Masters papers eventually, but then left the sea in favour of working in the family business, also specialising in production and sale of cod liver oil. This product, which used to be called "train oil" and was treasured as a product used in lamps as well as a fine lubricant, was no longer used for those purposes, other petroleum products having come along that were cheaper to make, and less pungent to use. But by then the health values of cod liver oil were well-publicised, so a new market had opened up. Even so, Robert wound up bankrupt in the 1880s and sought and received commissions as the Chairman of the local "Road Board" taking care of the maintenance of the one and only local highway, if it could be called such in those days. He was also a Returning Officer in the elections that occurred regularly and frequently after the advent of Responsible Government, meaning he must have known how to bite his tongue concerning his own political leanings. However, the thing most remembered about him and his wife Maria Victoria Matilda Winsor (another one of the same family; three brothers marrying three sisters) was the tragic death of almost their whole family in one diphtheria epidemic in the winter of 1878-79. These epidemics were commonplace in those days, but what was not so common was for a family of originally 9 children (one more was added after the tragedy) to be reduced to one in a single year. It was said that the local community was so in fear of this concentration of death in one place that they would not allow Maria, who was home alone with Robert away at sea, to leave the house. Instead, each child's body was passed through the window after it had died and was hastily buried by a lay minister, no ordained minister being willing to take the chance of becoming infected. The survivor of this shocking tragedy, Robertha, married a Le Messurier man, and so did her younger sister, Helena, who was born one year after that fateful winter. Again, there were so few Protestant merchant class families remaining on the Southern Shore by then that it was almost certain that two or more siblings from one family would marry siblings from one of these other families.

Priscilla Anne Morry

The last of three daughters to be named Priscilla Anne Morry survived to adulthood but then died relatively young at 36, a victim of childbirth, as was so often the cause of death for women in outport Newfoundland. She too married a Le Messurier man, William Warner Le Messurier, the brother of Peter Paint Le Messurier who had married her older sister Mary.

Esther Graham Morry

The last child of Matthew and Anne was another Esther Graham Morry. She died at age twelve, the cause of death unknown. She is buried in Forge Hill Cemetery close to the grave of her grandfather, Matthew Morry I, but where her parents are buried is a mystery. Their grave may be nearby and the stone could have tumbled due to the harsh climate or been vandalized. Rumours circulated for years that local villagers used to take the stones from the old cemeteries to use as doorsteps and other construction material. Indeed, it is true that one of the oldest gravestones in Ferryland, that of Sarah (Sept 2 1762-June 4, 1772), the daughter of the original Robert Carter who settled in Ferryland before 1750, and whose stone is now preserved at the Ferryland Museum, was for many years a conversation piece in the rec room of one of her descendants. But in this case, before being too quick to condemn, it should be understood that had it not been retrieved and protected by him, it would probably not exist at all today, let alone be in the pristine condition in which we find it.

Figure 48. Gravestone of Sarah Carter, Ferryland Museum

Of all the children of Matthew Morry II who lived long enough to marry, all but two married someone from either the Carter, Winsor or Le Messurier families. Matthew III married twice, to Elizabeth Chafe and then Elizabeth Coulman (who was a Carter descendant). But Henry Sweetland Morry somehow went terribly off course and married Mary (Minnie) Devereaux, an Irish Roman Catholic! One can well imagine how well that was accepted in the family and the village. Fortunately for the two of them, there was a non-denominational cemetery in Ferryland at the time of their deaths and they both wound up being buried there side by side.

And so, our story comes to an end. I could extend it to several more generations. The Morry family business did live on in Ferryland until the last owner, my uncle, William Minty Morry, was forced to sell it after the collapse of the Northern Cod Stock. But it never was my intention that this should be a complete recounting of the entire family history of the Morry clan of Newfoundland, ex Devon, right down to the present day. Such a project may be worthwhile for the sake of the descendants of this line but not for a broader audience and I may someday prepare a complete annotated history of the family for those interested.

Meantime, I hope that this book has proven interesting and useful to others, particularly those interested in the development and settlement of Newfoundland outports and those who are just now getting their feet wet in building their own family histories.

Explicit hoc totum;

Pro Christi da mihi potum!

(An anonymous professional scribe, the mid-1300s)

APPENDIX 1: LINEAGE CHART OF THE AUTHOR

Produced by Legacy

1

Christopher John MORRY
b. 25 May 1949, St. John's, Newfoundland and Labrador, Canada
d.

2

Thomas Graham MORRY V-Father
b. 4 Dec 1919, Ferryland, Newfoundland and Labrador, Canada
m. 6 Sep 1945, St. John's, Newfoundland and Labrador, Canada
d. 1 May 2008, Ottawa, Carleton, Ontario, Canada
Evelyn Mary WHEELER - Mother
b. 6 Nov 1917, St. John's, Newfoundland and Labrador, Canada
d. 2 Aug 2009, Ottawa, Carleton, Ontario, Canada

3

Pte. Howard Leopold MORRY RNR-Grandfather
b. 24 Jul 1885, Ferryland, Newfoundland and Labrador, Canada
m. 2 Jun 1915, Edinburgh, Midlothian, Scotland
d. 8 Feb 1972, Ferryland, Newfoundland and Labrador, Canada
Fredris Marion Powdrell MINTY - Grandmother
b. 3 Apr 1895, Edinburgh, Midlothian, Scotland
d. 15 Feb 1948, Ferryland, Newfoundland and Labrador, Canada

4

Pte. Thomas Graham MORRY III-Great-grandfather
b. 4 Dec 1849, Ferryland, Newfoundland and Labrador, Canada
m. 1 Jun 1880, Renews, Newfoundland and Labrador, Canada
d. 24 Jul 1935, Victoria, British Columbia, Canada
Catherine Frances WHITE - Great-grandmother
b. 20 Aug 1852, Ferryland, Newfoundland and Labrador, Canada

d. 27 Aug 1927, Mount Pearl, Newfoundland and Labrador, Canada

5

John Henry MORRY-2nd great-grandfather
b. 23 Feb 1818, Calvert, Newfoundland and Labrador, Canada
m. 12 Dec 1848, Ferryland, Newfoundland and Labrador, Canada
d. 15 Apr 1897, St. John's, Newfoundland and Labrador, Canada
Elizabeth Sarah WINSOR - 2nd great-grandmother
b. 8 Sep 1827, Aquaforte, Newfoundland and Labrador, Canada
d. 13 Feb 1879, Ferryland, Newfoundland and Labrador, Canada

6

Matthew MORRY II JP-3rd great-grandfather
b. 27 Mar 1790, Dartmouth, Devon, England
m. Cir 1811, Ferryland, Newfoundland and Labrador, Canada
d. 19 Jun 1856, Calvert, Newfoundland and Labrador, Canada
Anne SANDERS - 3rd great-grandmother
b. 17 Mar 1790, Ferryland, Newfoundland and Labrador, Canada
d. 6 Jun 1867, St. John's, Newfoundland and Labrador, Canada

7

Capt. Matthew MORRY-4th great-grandfather
b. Bef 28 Mar 1750, Dartmouth, Devon, England
m. 1 Mar 1773, Dartmouth, Devon, England
d. 19 Jun 1836, Calvert, Newfoundland and Labrador, Canada
Mary GRAHAM - 4th great-grandmother
b. 2 Jun 1750, Dartmouth, Devon, England
d. 29 Oct 1796, Dartmouth, Devon, England

8

John MORY-5th great-grandfather
b. Cir 6 Oct 1711, Stoke Gabriel, Devon, England
m. 22 Dec 1736, Dartmouth, Devon, England
d. 16 Jul 1751, Dartmouth, Devon, England
Priscilla HARVEY - 5th great-grandmother
b. Cir 1715, Dartmouth, Devon, England
d. Bef 28 Jun 1765, Dartmouth, Devon, England

9

John MOREY-6th great-grandfather
b. Bef 24 Nov 1687, Stoke Gabriel, Devon, England
m. 7 Jan 1710, Stoke Gabriel, Devon, England
d. Bef 11 May 1772, Dartmouth, Devon, England
Elizabeth STONE - 6th great-grandmother
b. Cir 1682, Stoke Gabriel, Devon, England
d. Bef 12 Jun 1729, Stoke Gabriel, Devon, England

10

John MORY-7th great-grandfather
b. Bef 1 Jan 1663, Stoke Gabriel, Devon, England
m. 1680, Stoke Gabriel, Devon, England
d. Bef Feb 1736, Stoke Gabriel, Devon, England
Susanna - 7th great-grandmother
b. 1666, Devon, England
d. Bef 23 Feb 1736, Stoke Gabriel, Devon, England

11

William MORY-8th great-grandfather
b. Cir 1624, location unknown, presumed to be in Devon, England
m. 23 Sep 1650, Stoke Gabriel, Devon, England
d. Bef 20 Nov 1692, Stoke Gabriel, Devon, England
Jennet FULL - 8th great-grandmother
b. Bef 7 May 1626, Stoke Gabriel, Devon, England
d. Bef 1 Mar 1696, Stoke Gabriel, Devon, England

APPENDIX 2: FAMILY GROUP SHEETS

Family Group Record for William MORY
Produced by Legacy

Husband William MORY
AKA Willm MOORE, Willm MOREY, Will MORY, Willm MORY
Born Cir 1624 Stoke Gabriel, Devon, England
Christened Cir 1624 Stoke Gabriel, Devon, England
Died Bef 20 Nov 1692 Stoke Gabriel, Devon, England
Buried 20 Nov 1692 Stoke Gabriel, Devon, England
Marriage 23 Sep 1650 Stoke Gabriel, Devon, England

Wife Jennet FULL
AKA Gennett FULL, Jennetta FULL, Jennettae FULL, Jennett MOREY
Born Bef 7 May 1626 Stoke Gabriel, Devon, England
Christened 7 May 1626 Stoke Gabriel, Devon, England
Died Bef 1 Mar 1695/96[32] Stoke Gabriel, Devon, England
Buried 1 Mar 1695/96 Stoke Gabriel, Devon, England

---

[32] Note: England and its colonies retained the old system of dating in which the calendar year ended on March 24th and New Year's Day was March 25th long after the rest of the western world had made January 1st New Year's Day. For the purpose of this study, any dates prior to 1752 are "double-dated" (e.g. March 1 1696/97 means that the event actually occurred in 1697 by our modern calendar whilst the people of the day in England and Newfoundland would have considered that it occurred in 1696.

Father William FULL (Bef 1587-Bef 1634) Mother Jane LANE (Bef 1592-Bef 1626)

Children
1 F Ellenor MOREY
Born Cir 1650 Stoke Gabriel, Devon, England
Christened
Died
Buried
Spouse William WEEKS (Cir 1650-) Bef 1671 - Stoke Gabriel, Devon, England
2 F Alice MOREY
AKA Alice MOARY, Alce MOREY
Born Bef 20 Apr 1651 Stoke Gabriel, Devon, England
Christened 20 Apr 1651 Stoke Gabriel, Devon, England
Died Bef May 1707 Stoke Gabriel, Devon, England
Buried 23 May 1707 Stoke Gabriel, Devon, England
Spouse Did Not Marry
3 F Elizabeth MORY
AKA Elisabeth MORY
Born Bef 1 May 1653 Stoke Gabriel, Devon, England
Christened 1 May 1653 Stoke Gabriel, Devon, England
Died Bef 12 Jul 1714 Stoke Gabriel, Devon, England
Buried 12 Jul 1714 Stoke Gabriel, Devon, England
Spouse Thomas EFFORD (Bef 1642-Bef 1695) 17 Nov 1674 - Stoke Gabriel, Devon, England
4 F Philippa MORY
AKA Phillip MORY, Phillipa POOK
Born Bef 20 Mar 1654/55 Stoke Gabriel, Devon, England
Christened 20 Mar 1654/55 Stoke Gabriel, Devon, England
Died Bef 12 May 1730 Stoke Gabriel, Devon, England
Buried 12 May 1730 Stoke Gabriel, Devon, England
Spouse William PIKE (Bef 1655-Bef 1716) 8 Oct 1677 - Stoke Gabriel, Devon, England
5 F Marie MORY
AKA Marie MOORE
Born Bef 2 Feb 1656/57 Stoke Gabriel, Devon, England
Christened 2 Feb 1656/57 Stoke Gabriel, Devon, England
Died Bef 8 Oct 1671 Stoke Gabriel, Devon, England
Buried 8 Oct 1671 Stoke Gabriel, Devon, England
Spouse
6 F Juditha MORY
AKA Judith HAWK, Judith MORY
Born Cir 1658 Stoke Gabriel, Devon, England

Christened
Died Bef 13 Sep 1713 Stoke Gabriel, Devon, England
Buried 13 Sep 1713 Stoke Gabriel, Devon, England
Spouse Richard HAWKE (Bef 1650-Bef 1709) 4 Apr 1676 - Stoke Gabriel, Devon, England

7 F Mary MORY
Born Bef 27 Dec 1660 Stoke Gabriel, Devon, England
Christened 27 Dec 1660 Stoke Gabriel, Devon, England
Died Bef 6 Apr 1707 Stoke Gabriel, Devon, England
Buried 6 Apr 1707 Stoke Gabriel, Devon, England
Spouse Richard ADAMS (Bef 1655-Bef 1608) 9 Sep 1684 - Stoke Gabriel, Devon, England

8 M William MORY
AKA William MOREY
Born Bef 13 Jan 1660/61 Stoke Gabriel, Devon, England
Christened 13 Jan 1660/61 Stoke Gabriel, Devon, England
Died Bef 31 Aug 1718 Stoke Gabriel, Devon, England
Buried 31 Aug 1718 Stoke Gabriel, Devon, England
Spouse

9 M John MORY
Born Bef 1 Jan 1662/63 Stoke Gabriel, Devon, England
Christened 1 Jan 1662/63 Stoke Gabriel, Devon, England
Died Bef Feb 1735/36 Stoke Gabriel, Devon, England
Buried
Spouse Susanna (1666-Bef 1736) 1680 - Stoke Gabriel, Devon, England

10 F Joane MORY
Born Bef 28 Aug 1664 Stoke Gabriel, Devon, England
Christened 28 Aug 1664 Stoke Gabriel, Devon, England
Died
Buried
Spouse

11 M Thomas MORY
Born Bef 4 Mar 1667/68 Stoke Gabriel, Devon, England
Christened 4 Mar 1667/68 Stoke Gabriel, Devon, England
Died
Buried
Spouse Elizabeth TAYLOR (Cir 1671-) 7 Oct 1688 - Exeter, Devon, England

12 F Jeane MORY
Born 1669 Stoke Gabriel, Devon, England
Christened 1669 Stoke Gabriel, Devon, England
Died Bef 5 Oct 1671 Stoke Gabriel, Devon, England
Buried 5 Oct 1671 Stoke Gabriel, Devon, England
Spouse Did Not Marry
Last Modified: 29 Jul 2017

Family Group Record for John MORY (1663-1736)
Produced by Legacy

Husband John MORY
Born Bef 1 Jan 1663 Stoke Gabriel, Devon, England
Christened 1 Jan 1663 Stoke Gabriel, Devon, England
Died Bef Feb 1736 Stoke Gabriel, Devon, England
Buried
Father William MORY (Cir 1624-Bef 1692) Mother Jennet FULL (Bef 1626-Bef 1696)
Marriage 1680 Stoke Gabriel, Devon, England

Wife Susanna
Born 1666 Devon, England
Christened
Died Bef 23 Feb 1736 Stoke Gabriel, Devon, England
Buried 23 Feb 1736 Stoke Gabriel, Devon, England

Children
1 F Gennet MORY
Born Bef 23 May 1682 Stoke Gabriel, Devon, England
Christened 23 May 1682 Stoke Gabriel, Devon, England
Died
Buried
Spouse

2 F Susanna MORY
Born 1683 Stoke Gabriel, Devon, England
Christened 1683 Stoke Gabriel, Devon, England
Died Bef 2 Sep 1755 Stoke Gabriel, Devon, England
Buried 2 Sep 1755 Stoke Gabriel, Devon, England
Spouse Robert HAWKE (Bef 1681-Bef 1731) 13 Aug 1706 - Stoke Gabriel, Devon, England

3 F Margaret MORY
AKA Margaret MOARY
Born Bef 14 Dec 1684 Stoke Gabriel, Devon, England
Christened 14 Dec 1684 Stoke Gabriel, Devon, England
Died Bef 30 Mar 1718 Stoke Gabriel, Devon, England
Buried 30 Mar 1718 Stoke Gabriel, Devon, England

Spouse Did Not Marry
4 M John MOREY
AKA John MOARY, John MORY, John MOURY
Born Bef 24 Nov 1687 Stoke Gabriel, Devon, England
Christened 24 Nov 1687 Stoke Gabriel, Devon, England
Died Bef 11 May 1772 Dartmouth, Devon, England
Buried 11 May 1772 Dartmouth, Devon, England
Spouse Elizabeth STONE (Cir 1682-Bef 1729) 7 Jan 1710 - Stoke Gabriel, Devon, England
Spouse Elizabeth MATTHEWS (Bef 1691-Bef 1763) 5 Feb 1732 - Dartmouth, Devon, England
5 M George MORY
Born Bef 9 Feb 1689 Stoke Gabriel, Devon, England
Christened 9 Feb 1689 Stoke Gabriel, Devon, England
Died
Buried
Spouse Elizabeth (-) Cir 1715 - Stoke Gabriel, Devon, England
6 F Mary MORY
AKA Mary MOREY
Born Cir 1691 Stoke Gabriel, Devon, England
Christened
Died Cir 1693 Stoke Gabriel, Devon, England
Buried 16 Jul 1693 Stoke Gabriel, Devon, England
Spouse
7 M William MORY
AKA William MOURY
Born Bef 9 Apr 1693 Stoke Gabriel, Devon, England
Christened 9 Apr 1693 Stoke Gabriel, Devon, England
Died Bef 25 Feb 1730 Dartmouth, Devon, England
Buried 25 Feb 1730 Stoke Gabriel, Devon, England
Spouse Joan FOGWELL (-) 6 Oct 1717 - Stoke Gabriel, Devon, England

Family Group Record for John MOREY (1687-1772)
Produced by Legacy

Husband John MOREY
AKA John MOARY, John MORY, John MOURY
Born bef 24 Nov 1687 Stoke Gabriel, Devon, England
Christened 24 Nov 1687 Stoke Gabriel, Devon, England

Died Bef 11 May 1772 Dartmouth, Devon, England
Buried 11 May 1772 Dartmouth, Devon, England
Father John MORY (Bef 1663-Bef 1736) Mother Susanna (1666-Bef 1736)
Marriage 7 Jan 1710/11 Stoke Gabriel, Devon, England
Other Spouse Elizabeth MATTHEWS (Bef 1697-Bef 1763) 5 Feb 1731/32 - Dartmouth, Devon, England

Wife Elizabeth STONE
Born Cir 1682 Stoke Gabriel, Devon, England
Christened
Died Bef 12 Jun 1729 Devon, England
Buried 12 Jun 1729 Stoke Gabriel, Devon, England

Children
1 M John MORY
AKA John MOREY
Born Cir 6 Oct 1711 Stoke Gabriel, Devon, England
Christened 6 Oct 1711 Stoke Gabriel, Devon, England
Died 16 Jul 1751 Dartmouth, Devon, England
Buried 29 Jul 1751 Dartmouth, Devon, England
Spouse Priscilla HARVEY (Cir 1715-Bef 1765) 22 Dec 1736 - Dartmouth, Devon, England

2 F Mary MORY
AKA Mary MOREY
Born bef 2 Dec 1712 Stoke Gabriel, Devon, England
Christened 2 Dec 1712 Stoke Gabriel, Devon, England
Died
Buried
Spouse John HARVEY (1708-) 26 Dec 1732 - Dartmouth, Devon, England

3 F Joan MOARY
AKA Joan MOREY
Born bef 7 Sep 1714 Stoke Gabriel, Devon, England
Christened 7 Sep 1714 Stoke Gabriel, Devon, England
Died Bef 2 Apr 1716 Stoke Gabriel, Devon, England
Buried 2 Apr 1716 Stoke Gabriel, Devon, England
Spouse Did Not Marry

4 F Joan MOARY
Born bef 7 Sep 1717 Stoke Gabriel, Devon, England
Christened 7 Sep 1717 Stoke Gabriel, Devon, England
Died
Buried
Spouse John STREET (-) 15 Jan 1738/39 - Stoke Gabriel, Devon, England

5 F Susanna MOARY
AKA Susanna MOREY
Born bef 12 Nov 1718 Stoke Gabriel, Devon, England
Christened 12 Nov 1718 Stoke Gabriel, Devon, England
Died
Buried
Spouse

6 M William MOARY
AKA William MOREY
Born bef 14 Aug 1720 Stoke Gabriel, Devon, England
Christened 14 Aug 1720 Stoke Gabriel, Devon, England
Died Bef 25 Feb 1729/30 Dartmouth, Devon, England
Buried 25 Feb 1729/30 Stoke Gabriel, Devon, England
Spouse Did Not Marry

7 M Richard MOARY
AKA Richard MOREY
Born bef 13 Jul 1722 Stoke Gabriel, Devon, England
Christened 13 Jul 1722 Stoke Gabriel, Devon, England
Died
Buried
Spouse Mary BLACKLER (-Bef 1820) 23 May 1749 - Dartmouth, Devon, England

8 F Jennet MOARY
Born bef 9 Sep 1724 Stoke Gabriel, Devon, England
Christened 9 Sep 1724 Stoke Gabriel, Devon, England
Died
Buried
Spouse

9 M Mathew MOARY
Born bef 29 Dec 1725 Stoke Gabriel, Devon, England
Christened 29 Dec 1725 Stoke Gabriel, Devon, England
Died
Buried
Spouse

10 F Jane MOREY
Born 1727 Dartmouth, Devon, England
Christened 29 Oct 1727 Dartmouth, Devon, England
Died Bef 8 Mar 1728/29 Dartmouth, Devon, England
Buried 8 Mar 1728/29 Dartmouth, Devon, England
Spouse Did Not Marry

11 F Elizabeth MOREY
Born bef 29 Oct 1729 Dartmouth, Devon, England
Christened 29 Oct 1729 Dartmouth, Devon, England
Died
Buried

Spouse Jasper STEER (1725-) 26 Dec 1749 - Dartmouth, Devon, England
Last Modified: 26 Jul 2017

Family Group Record for John MOREY (1687-1772)
Produced by Legacy

Husband John MOREY
AKA John MOARY, John MORY, John MOURY
Born bef 24 Nov 1687 Stoke Gabriel, Devon, England
Christened 24 Nov 1687 Stoke Gabriel, Devon, England
Died Bef 11 May 1772 Dartmouth, Devon, England
Buried 11 May 1772 Dartmouth, Devon, England
Father John MORY (Bef 1663-Bef 1736) Mother Susanna (1666-Bef 1736)
Marriage 5 Feb 1731/32 Dartmouth, Devon, England
Other Spouse Elizabeth STONE (Cir 1682-Bef 1729) 7 Jan 1710/11 - Stoke Gabriel, Devon, England

Wife Elizabeth MATTHEWS
AKA Elizabeth MATHEWS
Born bef 21 Nov 1697 Dartmouth, Devon, England
Christened 21 Nov 1697 Dartmouth, Devon, England
Died Bef 14 Mar 1763 Dartmouth, Devon, England
Buried 14 Mar 1763 Dartmouth, Devon, England
Father Roger MATHEWS (-) Mother

Children

1 F Sarah MOREY
Born bef 22 Jan 1732/33 Dartmouth, Devon, England
Christened 22 Jan 1732/33 Dartmouth, Devon, England
Died
Buried 16 Nov 1751 Dartmouth, Devon, England
Spouse

2 F Joan MOREY
Born bef 14 Jan 1734/35 Dartmouth, Devon, England
Christened 14 Jan 1734/35 Dartmouth, Devon, England
Died
Buried
Spouse

3 F Mary MORRY
Born Cir 1742 Dartmouth, Devon, England
Christened
Died Bef 8 Oct 1820 Dartmouth, Devon, England
Buried 8 Oct 1820 Dartmouth, Devon, England
Spouse
Last Modified: 26 Jul 2017

Family Group Record for John MOREY Jr. (1711-1751)
Produced by Legacy

Husband John MOREY Jr.
AKA John MOARY, John MORY
Born Cir 6 Oct 1711 Stoke Gabriel, Devon, England
Christened 6 Oct 1711 Stoke Gabriel, Devon, England
Died 16 Jul 1751 Dartmouth, Devon, England
Buried 29 Jul 1751 Dartmouth, Devon, England
Father John MOREY (Bef 1687-Bef 1772) Mother Elizabeth STONE (Cir 1682-Bef 1729)
Marriage 22 Dec 1736 Dartmouth, Devon, England

Wife Priscilla HARVEY
Born Cir 1715 Dartmouth, Devon, England
Christened
Died Bef 28 Jun 1765 Dartmouth, Devon, England
Buried 28 Jun 1765 Dartmouth, Devon, England
Father HARVEY (-) Mother

Children
1 M John MOREY
AKA John MORRY
Born bef 9 Nov 1737 Dartmouth, Devon, England
Christened 9 Nov 1737 Dartmouth, Devon, England
Died 15 Feb 1766 Dartmouth, Devon, England
Buried 26 Feb 1766 Dartmouth, Devon, England
Spouse Did Not Marry
2 F Priscilla MOREY

Born bef 30 Nov 1738 Dartmouth, Devon, England
Christened 30 Nov 1738 Dartmouth, Devon, England
Died 21 Dec 1738 Dartmouth, Devon, England
Buried After 21 Dec 1738 Dartmouth, Devon, England
Spouse Did Not Marry
3 M William MOREY
Born 2 Jan 1738/39 Dartmouth, Devon, England
Christened 2 Jan 1738/39 Dartmouth, Devon, England
Died Bef 8 Feb 1738/39 Dartmouth, Devon, England
Buried 8 Feb 1738/39 Dartmouth, Devon, England
Spouse Did Not Marry
4 M William MOREY
AKA William Thomas MOREY
Born bef 2 Jan 1739/40 Dartmouth, Devon, England
Christened 2 Jan 1739/40 Dartmouth, Devon, England
Died Bef 28 Jun 1741 Dartmouth, Devon, England
Buried 28 Jun 1741 Dartmouth, Devon, England
Spouse Did Not Marry
5 F Susannah MOREY
AKA Susanna MOREY
Born bef 19 Sep 1742 Dartmouth, Devon, England
Christened 19 Sep 1742 Dartmouth, Devon, England
Died Bef 28 Nov 1742 Dartmouth, Devon, England
Buried 28 Nov 1742 Dartmouth, Devon, England
Spouse Did Not Marry
6 F Elizabeth MORRY
AKA Elizabeth MOREY
Born bef 27 Mar 1744 Dartmouth, Devon, England
Christened 27 Mar 1744 Dartmouth, Devon, England
Died Bef 7 Sep 1831 Dartmouth, Devon, England
Buried 7 Sep 1831 Dartmouth, Devon, England
Spouse Samuel HOYLES (1748-) 2 Aug 1776 - Dartmouth, Devon, England
7 M Capt. Matthew MORRY
AKA Matthew MOREY
Born bef 28 Mar 1750 Dartmouth, Devon, England
Christened 28 Mar 1750 Dartmouth, Devon, England
Died 19 Jun 1836 Calvert, Newfoundland and Labrador, Canada
Buried 29 Jun 1836 Ferryland, Newfoundland and Labrador, Canada
Spouse Mary GRAHAM (1750-1796) 1 Mar 1773 - Dartmouth, Devon, England
Spouse Anne CARTER (1750-Bef 1838) After 1813 - St. John's, Newfoundland and Labrador, Canada
Last Modified: 30 Jul 2017

Family Group Record for Capt. Matthew MORRY I (1750-1836)
Produced by Legacy

Husband Capt. Matthew MORRY
AKA Matthew MOREY
Born bef 28 Mar 1750 Dartmouth, Devon, England
Christened 28 Mar 1750 Dartmouth, Devon, England
Died 19 Jun 1836 Calvert, Newfoundland and Labrador, Canada
Buried 29 Jun 1836 Ferryland, Newfoundland and Labrador, Canada
Father John MOREY Jr. (Cir 1711-1751) Mother Priscilla HARVEY (Cir 1715-Bef 1765)
Marriage 1 Mar 1773 Dartmouth, Devon, England
Other Spouse Anne CARTER (1750-Bef 1838) After 1813 - St. John's, Newfoundland and Labrador, Canada

Wife Mary GRAHAM
Born 2 Jun 1750 Dartmouth, Devon, England
Christened 27 Jun 1750 Dartmouth, Devon, England
Died 29 Oct 1796 Dartmouth, Devon, England
Buried 3 Nov 1796 Dartmouth, Devon, England
Father Capt. Christopher GRAHAM (Cir 1721-) Mother Mary CHURCHWILL (Bef 1725-Bef 1817)

Children
1 M John MORRY
Born bef 1 Jan 1776 Dartmouth, Devon, England
Christened 1 Jan 1776 Dartmouth, Devon, England
Died Feb 1807 Dartmouth, Devon, England
Buried
Spouse Mary Foale LUKE (Bef 1770-Bef 1807) 11 May 1797 - Dartmouth, Devon, England
2 F Honour MOARY
Born bef 29 Dec 1778 St. John's, Newfoundland and Labrador, Canada
Christened 29 Dec 1778 St. John's, Newfoundland and Labrador, Canada
Died
Buried 26 Sep 1779 St. John's, Newfoundland and Labrador, Canada
Spouse Did Not Marry
3 F Priscilla Ann MORRY

Born 28 Mar 1783 Dartmouth, Devon, England
Christened 2 Apr 1783 Dartmouth, Devon, England
Died 19 Dec 1820 Dartmouth, Devon, England
Cause of Death Possibly died in childbirth; she had just borne a child that month
Buried 24 Dec 1820 Dartmouth, Devon, England
Spouse William SWEETLAND (1788-1864) 15 Feb 1810 - Dartmouth, Devon, England

4 M Thomas Graham MORRY I
Born bef 27 Oct 1786 St. Saviour's, Dartmouth, Devon, England
Christened 27 Oct 1786 St. Saviour's, Dartmouth, Devon, England
Died Cir 1807 Dartmouth, Devon, England
Buried
Spouse

5 F Mary MORRY
AKA Mary MOREY
Born bef 6 Oct 1789 Dartmouth, Devon, England
Christened 6 Oct 1789 Dartmouth, Devon, England
Died After 1851 Dartmouth, Devon, England
Buried
Spouse Arthur KEMP (Bef 1785-1848) 21 Nov 1811 - Dartmouth, Devon, England

6 M Matthew MORRY II JP
AKA Jonathan MORRY
Born 27 Mar 1790 Dartmouth, Devon, England
Christened 8 Apr 1791 St. Saviour's, Dartmouth, Devon, England
Died 19 Jun 1856 Calvert, Newfoundland and Labrador, Canada
Buried 29 Jun 1856 Ferryland, Newfoundland and Labrador, Canada
Spouse Anne SANDERS (1790-1867) Cir 1811 - Ferryland, Newfoundland and Labrador, Canada

7 F Esther Graham MORRY
AKA Esther G MOREY, Esther Graham MOREY, Hester MOREY, Hestor Graham MORRY
Born bef 23 Jan 1795 Dartmouth, Devon, England
Christened 23 Jan 1795 Dartmouth, Devon, England
Died 14 Oct 1866 Dartmouth, Devon, England
Buried
Spouse Did Not Marry
Last Modified: 30 Jul 2017

Family Group Record for Capt. Matthew MORRY I (1750-1836)
Produced by Legacy

Husband Capt. Matthew MORRY
AKA Matthew MOREY
Born bef 28 Mar 1750 Dartmouth, Devon, England
Christened 28 Mar 1750 Dartmouth, Devon, England
Died 19 Jun 1836 Calvert, Newfoundland and Labrador, Canada
Buried 29 Jun 1836 Ferryland, Newfoundland and Labrador, Canada
Father John MOREY Jr. (Cir 1711-1751) Mother Priscilla HARVEY (Cir 1715-Bef 1765)
Marriage After 1813 St. John's, Newfoundland and Labrador, Canada
Other Spouse Mary GRAHAM (1750-1796) 1 Mar 1773 - Dartmouth, Devon, England

Wife Anne CARTER
Born 17 Mar 1749/50 Ferryland, Newfoundland and Labrador, Canada
Christened
Died Bef 15 Sep 1838 Calvert, Newfoundland and Labrador, Canada
Buried 15 Sep 1838 Ferryland, Newfoundland and Labrador, Canada
Father Robert CARTER JP (1722-1800) Mother Ann WYLLY (Bef 1719-After 1800)
Other Spouse Capt. Samuel HILL (Bef 1748-Bef 1785) 1775 - Topsham, Devon, England
Other Spouse Capt. Henry J. SWEETLAND J. P. (1733-1791) Cir 1785 - Ferryland, Newfoundland and Labrador, Canada

Children
Last Modified: 30 Jul 2017

Family Group Record for Matthew MORRY II JP (1790-1856)
Produced by Legacy

APPENDIX 2 195

Husband Matthew MORRY II JP
AKA Jonathan MORRY
Born 27 Mar 1790 Dartmouth, Devon, England
Christened 8 Apr 1791 St. Saviour's, Dartmouth, Devon, England
Died 19 Jun 1856 Calvert, Newfoundland and Labrador, Canada
Buried 29 Jun 1856 Ferryland, Newfoundland and Labrador, Canada
Father Capt. Matthew MORRY (Bef 1750-1836) Mother Mary GRAHAM (1750-1796)
Marriage Cir 1811 Ferryland, Newfoundland and Labrador, Canada

Wife Anne SANDERS
Born 17 Mar 1790 Ferryland, Newfoundland and Labrador, Canada
Christened 4 Jun 1790 St. John's, Newfoundland and Labrador, Canada
Died 6 Jun 1867 St. John's, Newfoundland and Labrador, Canada
Cause of Death Unknown but ill for a long while
Buried 9 Jun 1867 St. John's, Newfoundland and Labrador, Canada
Father Daniel SANDERS (Cir 1752-1834) Mother Mary CARTER (-Bef 1800)

Children
1 M Thomas Graham MORRY II
AKA Thomas Graham MOREY
Born 24 Jun 1812 Calvert, Newfoundland and Labrador, Canada
Christened
Died Bef 18 Jan 1879 St. John's, Newfoundland and Labrador, Canada
Buried 18 Jan 1879 St. John's, Newfoundland and Labrador, Canada
Spouse Eliza Shirley Hutchings LE MESSURIER (Cir 1809-1892)
Marr. Date 25 Nov 1840 - St. John's, Newfoundland and Labrador, Canada
2 M Matthew MORRY III
AKA Matthew MOREY
Born 24 Aug 1813 Calvert, Newfoundland and Labrador, Canada
Christened
Died Bef 30 Jul 1854 Calvert, Newfoundland and Labrador, Canada
Buried 30 Jul 1854 Ferryland, Newfoundland and Labrador, Canada
Spouse Elizabeth CHAFE (1815-Bef 1838) 18 Jul 1838 - Petty Harbour, Newfoundland and Labrador, Canada
Spouse Elizabeth COULMAN (Cir 1813-1884) 19 Feb 1844 - Ferryland, Newfoundland and Labrador, Canada
3 M Capt. William Sweetland MORRY
AKA William Sweetland MOREY
Born 8 Sep 1814 Calvert, Newfoundland and Labrador, Canada
Christened
Died Bef 20 May 1892 Calvert, Newfoundland and Labrador, Canada

Buried 20 May 1892 Ferryland, Newfoundland and Labrador, Canada
Spouse Jane WINSOR (1819-1868) 29 Apr 1845 - Ferryland, Newfoundland and Labrador, Canada
4 F Mary MORRY
AKA Mary MOREY, Eliza Mary MORRY
Born 10 Jun 1816 Calvert, Newfoundland and Labrador, Canada
Christened 29 Sep 1818 St. John's, Newfoundland and Labrador, Canada
Died 19 Jan 1857 St. John's, Newfoundland and Labrador, Canada
Buried 24 Feb 1857 St. John's, Newfoundland and Labrador, Canada
Spouse Peter Paint LE MESSURIER (Cir 1812-1884) 7 Feb 1843 - Ferryland, Newfoundland and Labrador, Canada
5 M John Henry MORRY
AKA John MOREY, John MORRY
Born 23 Feb 1818 Calvert, Newfoundland and Labrador, Canada
Christened 29 Sep 1818 St. John's, Newfoundland and Labrador, Canada
Died 15 Apr 1897 St. John's, Newfoundland and Labrador, Canada
Buried 18 Apr 1897 Ferryland, Newfoundland and Labrador, Canada
Spouse Elizabeth Sarah WINSOR (1827-1879) 12 Dec 1848 - Ferryland, Newfoundland and Labrador, Canada
6 M Benjamin Sweetland MORRY
Born 11 Nov 1819 Calvert, Newfoundland and Labrador, Canada
Christened 27 Sep 1823 Ferryland, Newfoundland and Labrador, Canada
Died 17 Feb 1895 Ferryland, Newfoundland and Labrador, Canada
Buried 19 Feb 1895 Ferryland, Newfoundland and Labrador, Canada
Spouse Sarah Weston CARTER (1827-1893) 2 May 1850 - Ferryland, Newfoundland and Labrador, Canada
7 M Henry Sweetland MORRY
Born 1 Jun 1821 Calvert, Newfoundland and Labrador, Canada
Christened 27 Sep 1823 Ferryland, Newfoundland and Labrador, Canada
Died 11 Aug 1897 Shores Cove, Cape Broyle, Newfoundland and Labrador, Canada
Cause of Death Old Age
Buried After 11 Aug 1897 Ferryland, Newfoundland and Labrador, Canada
Spouse Mary DEVEREAUX (Cir 1831-1870) Cir 1850 - Ferryland, Newfoundland and Labrador, Canada
8 M Capt. Arthur Kemp MORRY
Born 9 Feb 1823 Calvert, Newfoundland and Labrador, Canada
Christened 12 Oct 1823 Ferryland, Newfoundland and Labrador, Canada
Died 16 Dec 1907 Ferryland, Newfoundland and Labrador, Canada
Cause of Death Old Age
Buried 18 Dec 1907 Ferryland, Newfoundland and Labrador, Canada
Spouse Mary Oxenham CARTER (1829-1895) 5 Nov 1852 - St. John's, Newfoundland and Labrador, Canada

9 F Priscilla Anne MORRY
Born bef 4 Oct 1825 Calvert, Newfoundland and Labrador, Canada
Christened 4 Oct 1825 Ferryland, Newfoundland and Labrador, Canada
Died Bef 1832 Calvert, Newfoundland and Labrador, Canada
Buried
Spouse Did Not Marry
10 M Frederick Clift MORRY
AKA Frederic Clift MORRY
Born 10 Jan 1827 Calvert, Newfoundland and Labrador, Canada
Christened 28 Aug 1827 Ferryland, Newfoundland and Labrador, Canada
Died After 15 Mar 1858 Indian Ocean
Cause of Death Drowning - Lost at Sea
Buried
Spouse
11 M George MORRY
Born 25 Sep 1828 Calvert, Newfoundland and Labrador, Canada
Christened 1 Oct 1828 Calvert, Newfoundland and Labrador, Canada
Died 4 Oct 1828 Ferryland, Newfoundland and Labrador, Canada
Buried After 4 Oct 1828 Ferryland, Newfoundland and Labrador, Canada
Spouse
12 F Priscilla Anne MORRY
Born bef 4 Oct 1828 Calvert, Newfoundland and Labrador, Canada
Christened 4 Oct 1828 Ferryland, Newfoundland and Labrador, Canada
Died Bef 1832 Calvert, Newfoundland and Labrador, Canada
Buried
Spouse
13 M Robert MORRY
Born 21 Nov 1829 Calvert, Newfoundland and Labrador, Canada
Christened 10 Jun 1831 Ferryland, Newfoundland and Labrador, Canada
Died 6 May 1898 Calvert, Newfoundland and Labrador, Canada
Buried
Spouse Maria Victoria Matilda WINSOR (1834-1906)
Marr. Date 19 Jun 1858 - St. John's, Newfoundland and Labrador, Canada
14 F Priscilla Ann MORRY
AKA Priscilla MORRY
Born bef 5 Dec 1832 Calvert, Newfoundland and Labrador, Canada
Christened 5 Dec 1832 Ferryland, Newfoundland and Labrador, Canada
Died 12 Jan 1868 St. John's, Newfoundland and Labrador, Canada
Cause of Death Effects of childbirth
Buried 25 Jan 1868 St. John's, Newfoundland and Labrador, Canada
Spouse William Warner LE MESSURIER (Bef 1819-Cir 1897)
Marr. Date 20 Jan 1858 - Ferryland, Newfoundland and Labrador, Canada
15 F Esther Graham MORRY
Born 7 Apr 1837 Calvert, Newfoundland and Labrador, Canada

Christened 30 Sep 1837 Ferryland, Newfoundland and Labrador, Canada
Died 25 Nov 1849 Calvert, Newfoundland and Labrador, Canada
Buried 2 Dec 1849 Ferryland, Newfoundland and Labrador, Canada
Spouse
Last Modified: 3 Aug 2017

APPENDIX 3: COURT CASES

Involving Matthew and John Foale Morry

His Majesty's High Court of Chancery

1. Morry v Rowe: C 13/1987/62. 3rd July 1811. Plaintiff: Matthew Morry. Defendant: Joshua Rowe. Bill only.

2. Morry v Newman: C 13/2148/31. 30th June 1819. Plaintiff: Matthew Morry. Defendants: Robert Newman, Walter Prideaux, Walter Were Prideaux and Robert Were Prideaux. Bill and Answer.

3. Morry v Newman: C 13/2148/32. 30th June 1819. Plaintiff: Matthew Morry. Defendants: Robert Newman, Walter Prideaux,

Walter Were Prideaux and Robert Were Prideaux. Bill and Answer.

4.Morry v Hunt: C 13/2148/39. 30th April 1819. Plaintiff: John Morry. Defendants: Walter Prideaux, Matthew Morry and William Cholwich Hunt. Bill and Three Answers.

6. Morry v Prideaux: C 13/1441/6. 22nd December 1820. Plaintiff: John Morry. Defendants: Matthew Morry and Walter Prideaux. Two sets of Depositions

Decrees and Orders on the Cases of John Foale Morry vs Walter Prideaux, Matthew Morry and William Cholwich Hunt

    a. IND 1-10699-36 C 33-663 folio 1406 Morry v Morry et al 22 June 1819

    b. IND 1-10699-40 C 33-684 folio 24 Morry v Prideaux et al 13 Nov 1820 and 20 Nov 1820

    c. IND 1-10699-40 C 33-684 folio 81 Morry v Prideaux et al ca Dec 1820

d. IND 1-10699-40 C 33-687 folio 1196 Morry v Prideaux et al   20 June 1821

e. IND 1-10699-40 C 33-687 folio 1345-1349 Morry v Prideaux et al   4 May 1821

f. IND 1-10699-44 C 33-711 folio 1188d Morry vs Prideaux et al   7 June 1823

g. IND 1-10699-44 C 33-711 folio 1288 Morry vs Prideaux et al   5 July 1823

h. IND 1-10699-46 C 33-720 folio 26 Morry vs Prideaux   18 Nov 1823

i. IND 1-10699-47 C 33-734 folio 1027-1028 Morry vs Prideaux   8 Mar 1825

j. IND 1-10699-48 C 33-736 folio 1530-1531 Morry vs Prideaux   26 Jul 1825

7. Morry v Prideaux: C 13/2155/2 1818-1819. Plaintiff: Matthew Morry. Defendants: Walter Prideaux and John Square. Two Bills and One Answer

Decrees and Orders on the Case of Matthew Morry vs Walter Prideaux and John Square

a. IND 1-10699-34 C 33-651 folio 1067 Morry v Prideaux & Square   June 18, 1818

b. IND 1-10699-34 C 33-651 folio 1228 Morry v Prideaux & Square   July 1, 1818

c. IND 1-10699-36 C 33-663 folio 1246 Merry v Prideaux & Square   June 15 1819

d. IND 1-10699-36 C 33-663 folio 1406 Morry v Prideaux et al   June 25, 1819

His Majesty's Court of King's Bench

1. KB 122-1002-1762 Prideaux and Prideaux vs Prideaux and Morry, 1818

2. KB 122-1011-1690 Britten & Olive vs Morry & Prideaux, 1819

3. KB 122-1020-2914 Newman vs Morry & Prideaux, 1819

4. KB 122-1033-781 Graham et al vs Prideaux, 1820

Supreme Court of Newfoundland and Southern District Court, Ferryland

1. Square v Matthew Morry & Co - GN 5-2-A-1 Supreme Court Central Minutes Box 28. 14 Sept. 1818

2. GN 5 1 C 1 52-54 John Square vs Matthew Morry & Co, 30 Sept. 18

REFERENCES

- **Barnable, Gerald; Curran, Christopher and Melvin Baker, Editors**; *A Ferryland Merchant-Magistrate – The Journal and Cases of Robert Carter, Es$^{q.}$ J.P. 1832-1840, Vol. 1 and 2*; Law Society of Newfoundland and Labrador, St. John's, NL; 2013-2014; ISBN: 978-1-926574-82-0 (Vol. 1) and 978-1-926574-98-1 (Vol. 2, Part 1 and 2)
- **Brown, Jonathan**; *Tracing Your Rural Ancestors – A Guide for Family Historians*; Pen & Sword Family Books Ltd., Barnsley, SY; 2011; ISBN: 978 1 84884 227 4
- **Campbell, Ginny**; *Dartmouth Through Time*; Amberley Publishing, Stroud, GLOS; 2014; ISBN: 978 1 4456 3347 3
- **Colvin, Tony and Jenny Pearson**; *Topsham to Newfoundland*; Topsham Museum Society, Topsham, DEV; 2017; Brochure published for the 2017 Devon-Newfoundland Story heritage event in cooperation with the Devonshire Association and the Devon Family History Society.
- **Cuff, Robert A., Managing Editor; Baker, Melvin and Robert D. W. Pitt, Associate Editors**; *Dictionary of Newfoundland and Labrador Biography*; Harry Cuff Publications Ltd., St. John's, NL; 1990; ISBN: 0-921191-51-0

- **Cuff, Robert et. al.**; *Newfoundland and Labrador – Insiders Perspective*; Johnson Family Foundation, St. John's, NL; 2001; ISBN: 0-9685672-1-5
- **Cuff, Robert H.**; *19th Century Newfoundland Outport Merchants*; Unpublished Manuscript submitted to Provincial Historic Commemorations Program; 2014
- **Durant, Will and Ariel**; *The Story of Civilization: Part VII – The Age of Louis XIV*; Simon and Schuster, New York, NY;1963; Library of Congress # 35-10016
- **Fardy, B. D.**; *Ferryland – The Colony of Avalonia*; Flanker Press, St. John's, NL; 2005; ISBN: 1-894463-78-1
- **Freeman, Ray**; *Dartmouth and its Neighbours*; Dart Books, Dartmouth, DEV; 1990; ISBN: 1 901536 00 9
- **Freeman, Ray and Eric Preston**; *John Davis 1543-1605 – The Master Navigator from the Dart*; Dartmouth History Research Group Paper 33, Dartmouth, DEV; 2007; ISBN: 1-899011-24-2
- **Galgay, Frank**, Compiled and Edited by; *A Pilgrimage of Faith – A History of the Southern Shore from Bay Bulls to St. Shott's*; Harry Cuff Publications Ltd., St. John's, NL; 1983; ISBN: 0-919095-54-2
- **Gray, Todd**, Edited with an Introduction by; *Early-Stuart Mariners and Shipping – The Maritime Surveys of Devon and Cornwall 1619-35*; Devon and Cornwall Record Society, New Series, Vol. 33, Exeter, DEV; 1990; ISBN: 0 901853 33 X
- **Guigné, Anna Kearney**, edited by; *The Forgotten Songs of the Newfoundland Outports - As Taken from Kenneth Peacock's Newfoundland Field Collection, 1951–1961*; University of Ottawa Press, Ottawa, ON; 2016; ISBN-13: 978-0776623849

- **Handcock, Gordon**; *The Story of Trinity*; Trinity Historical Society, Trinity, NL; 1996; ISBN-13: 978-0981001708
- **Handcock, W. Gordon**; *Soe Longe As There Comes Noe Women: Origins of English Settlement in Newfoundland*; Global Heritage Press, Campbellville, ON; 2003; ISBN 1-894378-49-0
- **Hawkins, Abraham**; *Kingsbridge and Salcombe, with the Intermediate Estuary, Historically and Topographically Depicted*; R. Southwood, Kingsbridge, UK;1819
- **Head, C. Grant**; *Eighteenth Century Newfoundland: a geographer's perspective*; McClelland & Stewart Ltd., Toronto, ON; 1994; ISBN-13: 978-0771097997
- **Job, Robert Brown**; *John Job's Family – Devon-Newfoundland-Liverpool – 1730-1953*; Auto-published; 1954
- **Keough, Willeen**; *The Slender Thread - Irish Women on the Southern Avalon, 1750-1869*; Columbia University Press, New York, NY; 2008; ISBN: 978-0-231132-02-2
- **Major, Kevin**; *As Near To Heaven By Sea – A History of Newfoundland and Labrador*; Penguin Canada, Toronto, ON; 2001; ISBN: 0-14-027864-8
- **Mannion, John J.**; *Irish Settlements in Eastern Canada – A Study of Cultural Transfer and Adaptation*; Univ. of Toronto Press, Toronto, ON; 1978; ISBN: 0-8020-6371-3
- **Martin, Clement**; *The Devonshire Dialect*; Peninsula Press, Newton Abbot, DEV; 1973; ISBN: 1 872640 22 2
- **McCarthy, Mike**; *The Irish in Newfoundland 1600-1900 – Their Trials, Tribulations & Triumphs*; Creative Publishers, St. John's, NL; 1999; ISBN: 1-894294-01-1

- **Moyles, R. G.**; *Complaints is Many and Various, but the Odd Divil Likes it – Nineteenth Century Views of Newfoundland*; Peter Martin Assoc., Toronto, ON; 1975; ISBN: 0-88778-098-9
- **Newfoundland Historical Society** (now the Newfoundland and Labrador Historical Society); *A Short History of Newfoundland and Labrador;* Boulder Publications, St. John's, NL; 2008; ISBN: 978-0-9783381-8-3
- *Newman Papers; MG 482 – Newman and Hunt;* Provincial Archives Division, The Rooms Corporation; St. John's, NL
- **O'Flaherty, Patrick**; *Old Newfoundland – A History to 1843*; Long Beach Press, St. John's, NL; 1999; ISBN: 0-9680998-2-3
- **Peacock, Kenneth**, collected and edited by; *Songs of the Newfoundland Outports*; National Museum of Canada Bulletin No. 197, Anthropological Series No. 65; Queen's Printer, Ottawa; 1965
- **Pocius, Gerald L.**; *A Place to Belong – Community Order and Everyday Space in Calvert, Newfoundland*; McGill-Queens University Press, Montreal & Kingston, Canada; 1991; ISBN: 0-7735-2137-2 (paper)
- **Pope, Peter E.**; *Fish into Wine: The Newfoundland Plantation in the Seventeenth Century*; The University of North Carolina Press, Chapel Hill, NC; 2004; ISBN-13: 978-0807855768
- **Pope, Randell**; *Planters & Merchants: a History of Fortune Bay*; DRC Publishing, St. John's, NL; 2015; ISBN: 9781926689890
- **Poynter, F.N.L.**, Edited by; *The Journal of James Yonge (1647-1721)*: Plymouth Surgeon; London: Longman, Green & Co. Ltd.; 1963

- **Prideaux, R. M.**; *Prideaux – a West Country Clan*; Phillimore & Co. Ltd., Chichester, SSX; 1989; ISBN: 0 85033 674 0
- **Prowse, Judge D. W.**; *A History of Newfoundland from the English, Colonial and Foreign Records*; Originally Published by Macmillan and Co. London, UK, 1895; Re-Published by Boulder Publications, St. John's, NL; 2002; ISBN: 0-9730271-1-8 (paperback)
- **Rompkey, Ronald**, compiled and edited by; *Garrison Town to Commercial City – St. John's, Newfoundland, 1800 to 1900*; DRC Publishing, St. John's, NL; 2012; ISBN: 978-1-926689-44-9
- **Smart, Ivor H.**; *Dartmouth Industry and Banking – The Story From 1795 to 1925*; Dartmouth History Research Group Paper 18; Dartmouth History Research Group, Dartmouth, DEV; 1995; ISBN: 1899011080
- **Stephens, Sheila and Mike Patrick**; *The Early Families of the 25 Strand*; Topsham History Group, Topsham, DEV; 2017; Brochure published for the 2017 Devon-Newfoundland Story heritage event in cooperation with the Devonshire Association and the Devon Family History Society.
- **Story, George M.**, Chairman, Editorial Board; *Encyclopedia of Newfoundland and Labrador*; Joseph R. Smallwood Heritage Foundation Inc.; Harry Cuff Publications Ltd., St. John's, NL; 1993; ISBN: 0-9693422-1-7 (set)
- **White, William**; *History, Gazetteer, and Directory of Devonshire, and the City and County of the City of Exeter*; Printed by Robert Leader for W. White; 1850

- **Wilcox, Martin**; *Fishing and Fishermen – A Guide for Family Historians*; Pen & Sword Family Books Ltd., Barnsley, SY; 2009; ISBN: 978 1 84415 988 8

AUTHOR'S BIOGRAPHY

This is the second foray into the field of historical writing by the author who, having been educated and trained in the environmental sciences, and having worked in that field for over forty years, has produced scores of scientific and technical papers, book chapters and research and science policy monographs.

His first historical narrative, "When the Great Red Dawn is Shining" (2014), concerned the experiences of his grandfather, Howard Leopold Morry, as an ordinary foot soldier in the Royal Newfoundland Regiment during the horrors of warfare in Gallipoli, on the Somme and in Ypres during WWI. This second book contains the essence of his 25 years of research on his own family, the Morrys of Devon and Newfoundland, as a model of the group of small to medium-scale merchants from the "West Country" who came at the very end of colonial exploitation of the Newfoundland cod fishery and chose to remain in their adopted home.

www.ingramcontent.com/pod-product-compliance
Lightning Source LLC
Chambersburg PA
CBHW072152100526
44589CB00015B/2194